place
and
placelessness

E Relph

Research in Planning and Design

Series editor Allen J Scott

1 **Place and placelessness** E Relph
2 **Environmentalism** T O'Riordan
3 **The 'new' urban economics** H W Richardson
4 **The automated architect** N Cross

p **Pion Limited, 207 Brondesbury Park, London NW2 5JN**

place
and
placelessness

E Relph

Pion Limited, 207 Brondesbury Park, London NW2 5JN

© 1976 Pion Limited
Reprinted 1980

ISBN 0 85086 055 5

Printed in Great Britain

Preface

Much of the recent discussion on environmental issues I have found both unsatisfactory and disquieting. Unsatisfactory because the analyses of behaviour or of particular problems are so frequently mechanical and abstract, simplifying the world into easily represented structures or models that ignore much of the subtlety and significance of everyday experience. Disquieting because these simplified structures often then serve as the basis for proposals for the design of environments and the manipulation of people and places into patterns that are supposed to be more efficient. These discussions are usually couched in the scientific terms of objectivity, fact, and theory which appear to have become widely accepted as the *only* valid and rigorous terms for explaining and resolving environmental problems.

This book has been written, if not exactly in opposition to these types of studies, at least as an attempt to participate in the development of an alternative approach to understanding environment. It is concerned not with abstract models and theories, but with the 'lived-world', with the settings and situations we live in, know and experience directly in going about our day to day activities. Specifically it is an examination of one phenomenon of the lived-world—place, and attempts to elucidate the diversity and intensity of our experiences of place. Place and sense of place do not lend themselves to scientific analysis for they are inextricably bound up with all the hopes, frustrations, and confusions of life, and possibly because of this social scientists have avoided these topics. Indeed the phenomenon of place has been the subject of almost no detailed discussion, although philosophers, historians, architects, and geographers have made brief comments about it.

In this book one of my main aims has been to identify the variety of ways in which places are experienced, and to do this four main themes have been developed. First, the relationships between space and place are examined in order to demonstrate the range of place experiences and concepts. Second, the different components and intensities of place experience are explored, and it is argued that there are profound psychological links between people and the places which they live in and experience. Third, the nature of the identity *of* places and the identity of people *with* places is analysed; and fourth, the ways in which sense of place and attachment to place are manifest in the making of places and landscapes are illustrated. The essence of the argument relating these themes is that distinctive and diverse places are manifestations of a deeply felt involvement with those places by the people who live in them, and that for many such a profound attachment to place is as necessary and significant as a close relationship with other people. It is therefore disturbing that so much planning and remaking of landscapes proceeds apparently in ignorance of the importance of place, even though the protests of the expropriated and uprooted demonstrate this very importance.

It would not be realistic to investigate the phenomenon of place without attending to the parallel phenomenon of placelessness—that is, the casual eradication of distinctive places and the making of standardised landscapes that results from an insensitivity to the significance of place. Part of this book is therefore an examination of the attitudes of placelessness and of the manifestations of these attitudes in landscapes.

The philosophical foundation for this study of place and placelessness is phenomenology—a philosophical tradition that takes as its starting point the phenomena of the lived-world of immediate experience, and then seeks to clarify these in a rigorous way by careful observation and description. Phenomenological methods have been used in a wide range of disciplines, including sociology, anthropology, psychology, theology, ethology, and biology, and have in these cases been developed as a viable alternative to approaches based on the philosophy of science. Yet in geography, in planning, and in architecture there have been no more than a handful of discussions concerning the relevance of phenomenological methods. In its application of phenomenological procedures to the phenomenon of place this book does therefore constitute a deliberate attempt to develop an alternative and philosophically well founded way of studying environment. This may not always be obvious because the technical language of phenomenology is avoided wherever possible, but the ideas and methods of phenomenology are implicit throughout the book, and are largely responsible for its structure.

Partly because my academic training has been in geography and partly because geographers have frequently held that place is central to their discipline, this book begins in geography. But the arguments developed and the phenomena examined have a much wider relevance than the discipline of geography. Architects, landscape architects, planners, and all those engaged in the investigation or design of environments, landscapes, or places can perhaps find something of interest here. And while the language and ideas are certainly academic, this book should have something to offer to anyone who feels an identity with a place, who appreciates a diversity of landscapes, or who is concerned about the on-going erosion of the distinctive places of the world.

Edward Relph
The Narth, Gwent and West Hill, Ontario
June 1975

Acknowledgements

This book is a substantially revised version of a doctoral thesis submitted at the University of Toronto in 1973. I wish to acknowledge the assistance of the following people in the preparation of that thesis, though they are not responsible for the subsequent modifications: Ken Hewitt, Joe May, Yi-fu Tuan, Allen Scott, Peter Cave (the terms 'disneyfication' and 'museumisation' are his), Chris Cassin, Joe Whitney, and Karl Francis. Zehra Alpar gave unfailing support in the lean years of graduate study; Audrey McCullough typed the manuscript quickly and accurately; David Harford of the Graphics Department of Scarborough College prepared the photographs from a motley collection of slides; the University of Toronto provided a welcome grant for the preparation of the manuscript. Irene, Alexa, and Gwyn not only made it all possible but also kept it in perspective. I also acknowledge that I am a lumper and borrower of ideas and that I have been influenced in various ways by the following places (in chronological order): Catbrook, The Narth, Monmouth and the Lower Wye Valley, Central London, Ealing, Exeter, the Annexe in Toronto and the great subtopia of Scarborough in Toronto. To these, and to all the people and places which have more fleetingly entered into my experience and influenced my thoughts, I am grateful.

Permission to reproduce illustrations has been given by the following publishers: George Allen and Unwin (figure 2.1); Michigan State University Press (figure 2.2); The Architectural Press and MIT Press (figure 2.3); Wadsworth and Department of Geography, Royal University of Lund (figure 2.5); Indiana University Press (figure 6.3); Public Archives of Ontario (figure 6.4); Wadsworth (figure 6.15); University of Pennsylvania Press (figure 6.16); figure 5.6 is reproduced with the permission of the Trustee of the Macnamara Collection and the Public Archives of Ontario. Figure 5.3 is by Lorna Farquharson and figure 5.5 by Michael Bunce; all other illustrations are the property of the author.

E Relph

Contents

1 Place and the phenomenological basis of geography 1
1.1 The concept of place 1
1.2 The phenomenological basis of geography 4
1.3 Aims and approaches 6

2 Space and place 8
2.1 Pragmatic or primitive space 8
2.2 Perceptual space 9
2.3 Existential space 12
    2.3.1 Sacred space 15
    2.3.2 Geographical space 16
    2.3.3 Structure of geographical space 18
2.4 Architectural space and planning space 22
2.5 Cognitive space 24
2.6 Abstract space 25
2.7 Relationships between the forms of space 26

3 The essence of place 29
3.1 Place and location 29
3.2 Place and landscape 30
3.3 Place and time 31
3.4 Place and community 33
3.5 Private and personal places 36
3.6 Rootedness and care for place 37
3.7 Home places as profound centres of human existence 39
3.8 The drudgery of place 41
3.9 Essence of place 42

4 On the identity of places 44
4.1 The identity of places 45
4.2 The components of the identity of places 46
4.3 Insideness and outsideness 49
    4.3.1 Existential outsideness 51
    4.3.2 Objective outsideness 51
    4.3.3 Incidental outsideness 52
    4.3.4 Vicarious insideness 52
    4.3.5 Behavioural insideness 53
    4.3.6 Empathetic insideness 54
    4.3.7 Existential insideness 55
4.4 Images and identities of places 56
    4.4.1 Individual images of place 56
    4.4.2 Group or community images of place 57
    4.4.3 Consensus and mass images of place 58
4.5 The development and maintenance of identities of places 59
4.6 Types of identities of places 61

5	**A sense of place and authentic place-making**	63
5.1	Authentic sense of place	64
	5.1.1 Unselfconscious sense of place	65
	5.1.2 Selfconscious sense of place	66
5.2	Authentically created places	67
	5.2.1 Places made unselfconsciously	68
	5.2.2 Places made selfconsciously	71
5.3	Authenticity and place	78
6	**Placelessness**	79
6.1	Inauthenticity	80
6.2	Inauthentic attitudes to place	82
	6.2.1 Kitsch	82
	6.2.2 Technique and planning	87
6.3	Placelessness	90
	6.3.1 Mass communication	90
	6.3.2 Mass culture	92
	6.3.3 Big business	109
	6.3.4 Central authority	114
	6.3.5 The economic system	115
6.4	The components of a placeless geography	117
7	**Experiences of the present-day landscape**	122
7.1	The distinctiveness of experiences of present-day landscapes	122
7.2	The landscape of reflection and reason	125
7.3	The absurd landscape	127
7.4	The mediating machine	129
7.5	The everyday landscape	131
7.6	Confusion and proteanism in present-day landscapes	133
7.7	The simple landscape	135
7.8	Significance in the present-day landscape	137
7.9	Concluding comments	139
8	**Prospects for places**	141
8.1	Place	141
8.2	Placelessness	143
8.3	The inevitability of placelessness?	144
8.4	Designing a lived-world of places	145
8.5	Conclusion	147
	References	149
	Subject and Author index	155

1

Place and the phenomenological basis of geography

1.1 The concept of place

"A knowledge of places", Hugh Prince (1961, p.22) has written, "is an indispensable link in the chain of knowledge". And in terms of the practical everyday knowledge that we need to organise our experiences of the world there can be little disputing this, for we have to know, differentiate, and respond to the various places where we work, relax, and sleep. But in itself this practical knowing of places, although essential to our existence, is quite superficial and is based mainly on the explicit functions that places have for us. That the significance of place in human experience goes far deeper than this is apparent in the actions of individuals and groups protecting *their* places against outside forces of destruction, or is known to anyone who has experienced homesickness and nostalgia for particular places. To be human is to live in a world that is filled with significant places: to be human is to have and to know *your* place. The philosopher Martin Heidegger (1958, p.19) declared that " 'place' places man in such a way that it reveals the external bonds of his existence and at the same time the depths of his freedom and reality". It is a profound and complex aspect of man's experience of the world.

The apparent importance of place, both functionally and existentially, has not been reflected in examinations of either the concept of place or of the nature of experience of place. Even architects and planners have displayed a distinct lack of interest; yet their task can be well understood as "the possession of place" (Lyndon, 1962, pp.33–34), as the "creation of place" (Gauldie, 1969, p.173), or as the development of a system of meaningful places that give form and structure to our experiences of the world (Norberg-Schulz, 1969, p.226). But perhaps more surprising than the uninterest of architects is the almost total failure of geographers to explore the concept of place, for the belief that the study of places is one of the particular concerns of geography has a long and well-established history. Writing at the beginning of the first century A.D. the geographer-historian Strabo (book II, chapter 5, section 17) was quite explicit about the duties of the geographer:

> "[S]ince different places exhibit different good and bad attributes, as also the advantages and inconveniences that result therefrom, some due to nature and some resulting from human design, the geographer should mention those which are due to nature, for they are permanent, whereas the adventitious attributes undergo changes. And also of the latter attributes he should indicate such as cannot persist and yet somehow possess a certain distinction and fame, which by enduring to later times make a work of man, even when it no longer exists, a kind of natural attribute of a place."

To whatever degree Strabo's advice was adopted, it is certainly the case that his brief comment remained until recently the most detailed statement on place in geography. This did not, however, prevent, the widespread use of the concept of place as a hopeful focus for the chronically divided discipline of geography. Consider, for example, the following aphoristic definitions by geographers—almost all without further explicit discussion of place:

> La géographie est la science des lieux et non celle des hommes (Vidal de la Blache, 1913, p.299).

> Geography is concerned with the association of things that give character to particular places (James, P., 1954, p.4).

> The facts of geography are place facts; their association gives rise to the concept of landscape (Sauer, 1963, p.321).

> The integrations which geography is concerned to analyse are those which vary from place to place (Hartshorne, 1959, p.15).

> Geography is the knowledge of the world as it exists in places (Lukermann, 1964, p.167).

And, following a tradition in the discipline of definition by committee, the Ad Hoc Committee on *The Science of Geography* suggested that "the modern science of geography derives its substance from man's sense of place and his curiosity about the spatial attributes of the surface and atmospheric envelope of the earth" (National Academy of Science, 1965, p.7). In concluding its report the committee reconsidered what was meant by sense of place and in a statement of quite remarkable reductionism observed that "... little is known as yet about what we earlier called the 'sense of place' in man. Its secrets are still locked from us in our inadequate knowledge of nervous systems. Someday, when the study of nervous systems has advanced sufficiently, a startling and perhaps revolutionary new input may reach geographical study in a full descriptive analysis of the sense of place" (National Academy of Science, 1965, pp.67–68).

Most geographers, then, seem to have been content if not to await patiently the appropriate advances in neurology at least to treat place as something intuitively obvious or as synonymous with region. But there are two brief discussions of the concept of place in geography (Lukermann, 1964; May, 1970) and these are significant because they serve to outline some of the features and confusions of the concept [1].

[1] A recent and important paper by Yi-fu Tuan (1975) makes it necessary to modify these comments. Tuan examines space and place in geography from a phenomenological perspective, and his arguments parallel and complement those presented in chapters 2 and 3 of this book. Hopefully the discussion here offers some different insights and ideas about the relationships between space and place and the nature of place itself, while generally reinforcing Tuan's humanist interpretations.

An analysis of the concept of place as it is used by Lukermann (1964) reveals six major components:

1. The idea of location, especially location as it relates to other things and places, is absolutely fundamental. Location can be described in terms of internal characteristics (site) and external connectivity to other locations (situation); thus places have spatial extension and an inside and outside.

2. Place involves an integration of elements of nature and culture; "each place has its own order, its special *ensemble*, which distinguishes it from the next place" (p.170). This clearly implies that every place is a unique entity.

3. Although every place is unique, they are interconnected by a system of spatial interactions and transfers; they are part of a framework of *circulation*.

4. Places are localised—they are parts of larger areas and are focuses in a system of localisation.

5. Places are emerging or becoming; with historical and cultural change new elements are added and old elements disappear. Thus places have a distinct historical component.

6. Places have meaning: they are characterised by the beliefs of man. "Geographers wish to understand not only why place is a factual event in human consciousness, but what beliefs people hold about place ... . It is this alone that underlies man's acts which are in turn what give character to a place" (p.169).

Thus Lukermann understands places as complex integrations of nature and culture that have developed and are developing in particular locations, and which are linked by flows of people and goods to other places. A place is not just the 'where' of something; it is the location plus everything that occupies that location seen as an integrated and meaningful phenomenon.

The concept of place is not, however, quite as coherent as this discussion perhaps implies. First of all it must be recognised, as May (1970, p.214) points out, that Lukermann does not distinguish clearly between the concepts of 'place', 'region', 'area', and 'location', and indeed uses these interchangeably. Hence he is preserving much of the confusion that is inherent in these terms and which has never been satisfactorily resolved by geographers, and is in effect bundling together a whole variety of different approaches and ideas. Taking a more analytic approach May points out that the notion 'place' has been used in three and perhaps four distinct senses by geographers. First, it has been used to refer to the entire surface of the earth, as for instance in the idea of the earth as the place of man. Second, it has been used to refer to a unit of space such as a city, province, or country, in which sense it cannot be clearly differentiated from 'region'. Third, it has been used to refer to a particular and specific part of space and to what may occupy that space, "as when we think of our place of residence as being a particular building or talk of a place of worship or a place of amusement". Finally, place has been used to mean 'location' in the sense of exact position, although strictly location is more specific than place, for "place is made up of a number of things that can be specifically located". May argues that only in the third of these senses is there something distinctive about the idea of place, for in this meaning place appears to possess some "perceptual unity" that is given to it by our experiences with unique and real places.

The confusion about the meaning of the notion of place appears to result because it is not just a formal concept awaiting precise definition, but is also a naive and variable expression of geographical experience. Consequently clarification cannot be achieved by imposing precise but arbitrary definitions, but must be sought by examining the links between place and the phenomenological foundations of geography—those direct experiences of the world which all formal geographical knowledge presupposes. This seems to be what May is hinting at when he suggests the importance of "perceptual unity" in place; it is also intimated by Lukermann (1964, p.168) when he writes that "the study of place is the subject matter of geography because consciousness of place is an immediately apparent part of reality, not a sophisticated thesis; knowledge of place is a simple fact of experience".

1.2 The phenomenological basis of geography
The foundations of geographical knowledge lie in the direct experiences and consciousness we have of the world we live in. This phenomenological basis for the discipline has been widely recognised by commentators on the nature of geography, but Paassen's statement (1957, p.21) is perhaps the most explicit and most succinct. He writes:

> Geographical science has in fact a phenomenological basis; that is to say, it derives from a geographical consciousness. On the one hand the geographer develops this consciousness and makes society more aware of geography, but on the other hand the rise of geographical science is dependent upon the existence of a prescientific and natural geographical consciousness ...; geographers and geography exist only in a society with a geographical sense.

Paassen does not explore this further, but his comments are echoed and developed by others. David Lowenthal (1961, p.242) suggests that "anyone who inspects the world around him is in some measure a geographer", and develops a geographical epistemology which is founded on personal geographies composed of direct experiences, memory, fantasy, present circumstances, and future purposes. It is these personal geographies that give meaning to formal academic geography. Thus it is that formal geography is, as Tuan (1971) has indicated, a mirror for man—reflecting and revealing human nature and seeking order and meaning in the experiences that we have of the world.

The most complete investigation of the direct experiences of the world that underlie geography is that made by Eric Dardel (1952) in his study of the nature of geographical reality. He argues that before any scientific geography there exists a profound relationship between man and the world he lives in—"une géographicité de l'homme comme mode de son existence et de son destin" (p.2). Geography is not to be understood as just another branch of knowledge with geographical reality being primarily an object and with geographical space a blank that is waiting to be filled in. Rather we should recognise that geographical reality is first of all the place where someone is, and perhaps the places and landscapes which they remember—formal concepts of location, region or landforms, are subsequent. It follows from this that geographical space is not uniform and homogeneous, but has its own name and is directly experienced as something substantial or comforting or perhaps menacing. It is the space of earth and rock, water and air, the built space of towns and villages, or landscapes expressing entire complexes of human intentions. In short, Dardel argues that geography is initially a profound and immediate experience of the world that is filled with meaning, and as such is the very basis of human existence. While geographical science may adopt an air of detachment, Dardel maintains that "it is necessary to understand geography not as some closed system where men submit themselves to observation like insects in a laboratory, but as the means by which man realises his existence insofar as the Earth is an essential aspect of his fate" (p.124).

Place has often been identified implicitly as the essential feature of the phenomenological foundations of geography. Thus Tuan (1961, p.30) declared that the first romance of geography comes through some real encounter with place, while de Martonne (cited in Dardel, 1952, p.28) suggested that geography is a response to a need to "fix the memory of the places which surround us", and Hartshorne (1959, pp.15, 115) states specifically that "it was to satisfy man's curiosity concerning the differences of the world from place to place that geography developed as a subject of popular interest". However, little that is substantial has been made of the interconnections between the phenomenological basis of geography and formal geographical knowledge that are manifest in place; instead attempts to clarify the concept of place have usually resulted in some tension or confusion between definition and experience. In this respect, place is simply reflecting the situation of all geography: "Geography, by its very position", writes Dardel (1952, p.133), "cannot avoid being stretched between knowledge and existence". There is a real possibility of geography solving such tension by abandoning itself to science and thus losing contact with its sources of meaning. It is precisely this loss of contact and this division that have been emphasised by a number of phenomenological philosophers. Thus Heidegger (1962, p.100) wrote that "the source which a geographer establishes for a river is not 'the springhead in the dale' ",

and Schütz (1967, p.466) observed that "the place in which I am living
has not significance as a geographical concept but as my home". More
explicit than these is Merleau-Ponty's statement (1962, p.ix) referring to a
world "which precedes knowledge, of which knowledge always speaks, and
in relation to which every scientific schematization is an abstract sign
language, as is geography in relation to the countryside in which we have
learnt beforehand what a forest, a prairie or a river is". In short, while
scientific geography can be understood as a response to our existential
involvement in the world, it is nevertheless far removed from the lived-
world in attempting to make man, space and nature objects of enquiry.
Furthermore, while place is often considered as a formal geographical
concept, any exploration of place as a phenomenon of direct experience
cannot be undertaken in the terms of formal geography nor can it solely
constitute part of such geography. It must, instead, be concerned with
the entire range of experiences through which we all know and make
places, and hence can be confined by the boundaries of no formally
defined discipline.

1.3 Aims and approaches
We live, act and orient ourselves in a world that is richly and profoundly
differentiated into places, yet at the same time we seem to have a meagre
understanding of the constitution of places and the ways in which we
experience them. At first glance this may seem paradoxical, but it is not,
for there is no need for knowledge to be explicit and selfconscious for it
to be valuable. Indeed most of the understanding we have of the realities
of everyday life is unselfconscious and not clearly structured (Berger and
Luckmann, 1967). But there is nevertheless a real problem in this lack of
formal knowledge of place. If places are indeed a fundamental aspect of
man's existence in the world, if they are sources of security and identity
for individuals and for groups of people, then it is important that the
means of experiencing, creating, and maintaining significant places are not
lost. Moreover there are many signs that these very means are disappearing
and that 'placelessness'—the weakening of distinct and diverse experiences
and identities of places—is now a dominant force. Such a trend marks a
major shift in the geographical bases of existence from a deep association
with places to rootlessness, a shift that, once recognised and clarified, may
be judged undesirable and possibly countered. It will then be of no small
importance to know what are the distinctive and essential features of place
and of our experiences of places, for without such knowledge it will not
be possible to create and preserve the places that are the significant contexts
of our lives.
   My purpose in this book is to explore place as a phenomenon of the
geography of the lived-world of our everyday experiences. I do not seek
to describe particular places in detail, nor to develop theories or models or
abstractions. Rather my concern is with the various ways in which places

manifest themselves in our experiences or consciousness of the lived-world, and with the distinctive and essential components of place and placelessness as they are expressed in landscapes.

The approach I adopt derives a great deal from phenomenological methods [2]. These proceed from an acceptance both of the wholeness and indivisibility of human experience, and of the fact that meaning defined by human intentions is central to all our existence. The lived-world and its geography are thus taken as being irrefutably and profoundly human and meaningful, and place can be approached with as few presuppositions as possible concerning its character or form, for it is recognised from the outset that place has a range of significances and identities that is as wide as the range of human consciousness of place.

[2] These methods are used implicitly rather than as explicit frameworks for description and analysis, for it is not the methodologies that are important here but the phenomenon of place. An account of phenomenological methods can be found in Spiegelberg (1965), but a clearer understanding of what these involve can be gained from instances where they have been used, for example in Berger and Luckmann, *The Social Construction of Reality* (1967); Berger *et al.*, *The Homeless Mind* (1973); the sociological essays of Alfred Schütz (1962); Hallowell's accounts (1955) of the life of Ojibway Indians; the analyses of perception and behaviour by Merleau-Ponty (1962, 1967); or Grene's survey (1965) of the use of phenomenological procedures by European biologists.

Space and place

The space we experience of sky or sea or landscape, or of a city spread out beneath us when viewed from a tall building, the built space of the street, of buildings viewed from the outside or experienced from the inside, the reasoned space of maps, plans, cosmographies, and geometries, interstellar space, the space possessed by objects or claimed by countries or devoted to the gods—this is the range of our experiences and understanding of space. Space is amorphous and intangible and not an entity that can be directly described and analysed. Yet, however we feel or know or explain space, there is nearly always some associated sense or concept of place. In general it seems that space provides the context for places but derives its meaning from particular places.

The nature of space has been the subject of much discussion by philosophers, scientists, and others (e.g. Jammer, 1969; Hawkins, 1964). These discussions have never been resolved and it is not easy to formulate any framework which embraces the variety of forms of space that have been identified and which is reasonably consistent. It would not be relevant to become involved in these debates, yet it is important to clarify the relations between space and place, and thus to avoid the separation of places from their conceptual and experiential context. This dilemma is sidestepped here somewhat arbitrarily by recognising that the various forms of space lie within a continuum that has direct experience at one extreme and abstract thought at the other extreme. Within this continuum certain types of space can be distinguished, for instance that of unselfconscious and pragmatic experiences, the selfconsciously experienced perceptual space of individuals, the built spaces of architecture, and the abstract space of geometry (cf Norberg-Schulz, 1971, pp.9-12). Of particular importance is 'existential' or 'lived' space, for this seems to be especially relevant to a phenomenological understanding of place. Of course, concepts or experiences or created spaces do not always fall neatly into one of these categories, and this classification is really only a heuristic device for clarifying space-place relationships. In this it is useful because it covers such a broad range of ideas, experiences, and activities involving space, and hence introduces some of the diverse meanings of place.

2.1 Pragmatic or primitive space
Primitive space is the space of instinctive behaviour and unselfconscious action in which we always act and move without reflection. This is an organic space that is rooted in things concrete and substantial and which involves no images or concepts of space and spatial relations. Such space is comparable to, and well characterised in terms of, the 'functional circle' of animals—that is, the environment in which animals survive and function but of which, so far as we can know, they have no abstract images.

Indeed primitive space is perhaps less well developed than functional circles for, as Ernst Cassirer (1970, pp.46–48) has pointed out, "a child has to learn many skills an animal is born with".

Primitive space is structured unselfconsciously by basic individual experiences, beginning in infancy, associated with the movement of the body and with the senses. It is these that provide the fundamental dimensions of left and right, above and below, in front of and behind, within reach and beyond reach, within hearing and beyond hearing, within sight and beyond sight (Tuan, 1974, pp.5–29). Since these experiences are common to almost everyone they are intersubjective and must be understood as not merely individual but as part of the basic spatial context of all cultural groups. They often achieve unwitting expression—Lévi-Strauss (1967, p.328) writes:

"... when a society is indifferent to space or a certain type of space (for instance, in our society, urban space when it has not been the object of planning), what happens is that unconscious structures seem to take advantage, as it were, of the indifference in order to invade the vacant area and assert themselves, symbolically or in actual fact ... . This applies both to the so-called primitive societies which appear to be indifferent to spatial expression and to more complex societies which profess the same attitude ..."

Thus there is the persistent theme of underworlds in cosmographies and in the social structure of the modern city, and there are front and back entrances to houses, villages, and towns (Tuan, 1971, p.187).

At this primitive level it is difficult to distinguish space and place. Perhaps space is simply a continuous series of egocentric places where things performing certain functions or meeting needs can be found, but of which no mental picture has formed. Spivak (1973, pp.33–46) has in fact suggested that there are some thirteen irreducible settings or 'archetypal places' required for unimpaired human behaviour. Each of these is identified with a significant whole behaviour, such as sleeping, feeding, excreting, playing, or sheltering. More remarkable is the proposal of Adolf Portmann (in Grene, 1965, pp.38–39), based on his careful observations of animals and insects, that these often display an attachment to secure and safe places that is so powerful that these places are best understood as *homes*. If Spivak and Portmann are correct then there is a deep and presymbolic differentiation of and attachment to place that is perhaps a biological rather than a peculiarly human characteristic, and it is only on the cultural and symbolic levels that place experience takes on a distinctively human quality.

2.2 Perceptual space
Man's inferiority to animals in terms of organic, primitive space is more than compensated for by his ability to reflect systematically on space and to experience it and encounter it selfconsciously. There is, of course, no

sudden leap from an organic involvement to sophisticated abstraction and
selfconsciousness; rather there are several levels of awareness and
abstraction. The most immediate form of awareness is that of 'perceptual
space'—the egocentric space perceived and confronted by each individual.
This is a space that has content and meaning, for it cannot be divorced
from experiences and intentions.

Perceptual space is a space of action centred on immediate needs and
practices, and as such it has a clearly developed structure. This is described
by Nitschke (cited in Norberg-Schulz, 1971, p.13): "Perceptual space has
a centre, which is perceiving man, and it therefore has an excellent system
of directions which change with the movement of the human body; it is
limited and in no sense neutral; in other words it is finite, heterogeneous
and subjectively defined and perceived; distances and directions are fixed
and relative to man." This structure can clearly be in no way understood
as objective or measurable—rather distances and directions are experienced
as qualities of near or far, this way or that, and even when these are made
explicit as paths or trails they are known with their special meaning.
Wallace Stegner (1962, pp.271–273) describes the satisfaction and delight
he experienced in wearing paths and tracks on his father's farm in
Saskatchewan: "... they were ceremonial, an insistence not only that we
had a right to be in sight on the prairie but that we owned and controlled
a piece of it ... . Wearing any such path in the earth's rind is an intimate
act, an act like love ...". Although not always with such clear expression
as this, in perceptual space each individual groups the world around him
as "a field of domination", and he singles out those elements which may
serve as a means or an end for his use or enjoyment. Theoretically it
might even be possible to draw contour lines of equal significance and
relevance for each individual (Schütz, 1962, Vol. 2, p.93). But these would,
of course, change as the individual's intentions and circumstances alter—just
as when we move to a new place of residence, the shops and streets that
were formerly so significant in our daily life cease to be of any importance.

Perceptual space is also the realm of direct emotional encounters with
the spaces of the earth, sea, and sky or with built and created spaces.
Matoré (1962, pp.22–23) writes: "We do not grasp space only by our
senses ... we live in it, we project our personality into it, we are tied to it
by emotional bonds; space is not just perceived ... it is lived." Space is
never empty but has content and substance that derive both from human
intention and imagination and from the character of the space. Such
'substantive space' is "the blue of the sky as a frontier between the visible
and the invisible; it is the emptiness of the desert, a space for death; it
is the frozen space of an ice bank; ... the depressing space of a heath in a
storm" (Dardel, 1952, p.10). It is also the 'telluric space' that we can
experience in the depth and solidity of the earth—"... a concrete and
immediate experience in which we feel the material intimacy of the crust
of the earth, a setting down of roots, a type of foundation for geographical

reality" (Dardel, 1952, p.20). It can be the mysterious, enclosing, intimate space of the forest (Bachelard, 1969, pp.185-189), or the spaces of water and air with their "shadows, reflections, haze and mist that dance lightly and blend our feelings with the fantasies of the world" (Dardel, 1952, p.31). And substantive space can also be experienced in any of the infinite variety of man-made spaces of buildings, streets, and landscapes (Tuan, 1974, pp.27-29). Such experiences of substantive space may sometimes be overwhelming or intense, as when we round a corner and come abruptly upon some magnificent view. Henry Miller (1947, p.343) describes such an experience: "My eye suddenly caught a view which took my breath away. From what was virtually an oubliette I was looking down on one of the oldest quarters of Paris. The vista was so sweepingly soft and intoxicating it brought tears to my eyes." More usually our experiences of perceptual space are fleeting and unexceptional, and accepted as part of the natural course of things. They are no less important for that, for it is these personal experiences of space that are the basis for much of the meaning that environments and landscapes have for us.

Through particular encounters and experiences perceptual space is richly differentiated into places, or centres of special personal significance. Paul Shepard (1967, p.32) suggests that for each individual "the organising of thinking, perception and meaning is intimately related to specific places", and no doubt we all have private places to which we can retreat in order to meditate. For children in particular, places constitute the basis for the discovery of the self, and caves or trees or even a corner of the house may be claimed as 'my place' (Cobb, 1970). These childhood places frequently take on great significance and are remembered with reverence; thus Albert Camus found that the memory of the ruins of Tipasa which he knew as a child provided an ongoing source of stability and meaning for him (Camus, 1955). Both remembered and currently significant places are essentially concentrations of meaning and intention within the broader structure of perceptual space. They are fundamental elements of the lived-geography of the world. Dardel (1952, p.46) writes: "For man geographical reality is first of all the place he is in, the places of his childhood, the environment which summons him to its presence."

Although they are personal, perceptual spaces and places are not entirely isolated within the individual, for there are common landscapes that are experienced. Teilhard de Chardin (1955, pp.6-7) wrote:

"It is tiresome and even humbling for the observer to carry with him everywhere the centre of the landscape he is crossing. But ... when chance directs his step to a point of vantage from which things themselves radiate (a crossroads or radiating valleys) ... the subjective viewpoint coincides with the way things are distributed objectively, and perception yields its apogee. The landscape lights up and yields its secrets. He sees."

But perhaps a more common and significant means of release from the
isolation of perceptual space is given by the intersubjective linking of
culture, experience, and intention. Indeed in terms of intersubjectivity
perceptual space is scarcely isolated at all—not only is it accessible through
empathetic understanding, but, as Alfred Schütz (1962, Vol.I, p.133) states:

> "Our everyday world is, from the outset, an intersubjective world of
> culture. It is intersubjective because we live in it as men among other
> men, bound to them through common influence and work, understanding
> others and being an object of understanding for others. It is a world of
> culture because, from the outset, the life-world is a universe of
> significations to us, i.e. a framework of meaning (*Sinnzussamenhang*)
> which we have to interpret, and of interrelations of meaning which we
> institute only through our action in the life-world."

In short, the individual is not merely in his own place at the centre of his
own space, but recognises from the start that all other individuals have
their perceptual spaces and places. Furthermore he is aware that these
constitute just part of the more or less agreed on and consistent lived-
space of the entire social or cultural group of which he is a member.

2.3 Existential space

Existential or lived-space is the inner structure of space as it appears to us
in our concrete experiences of the world as members of a cultural group
(Bollnow, 1967; Schütz, 1962, Vol.II, pp.122–127). It is intersubjective
and hence amenable to all members of that group for they have all been
socialised according to a common set of experiences, signs, and symbols
(Berger and Luckmann, 1967, pp.130–131). The meanings of existential
space are therefore those of a culture as experienced by an individual,
rather than a summation of the meanings of individual perceptual spaces,
though in many cases the two probably coincide. Furthermore existential
space is not merely a passive space waiting to be experienced, but is
constantly being created and remade by human activities. It is the space
in which "human intention inscribes itself on the earth" (Dardel, 1952,
p.40), and in so doing creates unselfconsciously patterns and structures of
significance through the building of towns, villages, and houses, and the
making of landscapes.
    An example given by Lévi-Strauss (1967, pp.132–133) will serve to
demonstrate something of the character of existential space, and while
this is an ideal type taken from a non-literate culture, similar though less
clearly defined forms are to be found in all cultures. The village plan of
Omarakana in the Trobriand Islands is arranged in concentric rings around
a central public plaza (figure 2.1). The inner ring consists of yam storage
houses, sacred and the object of many taboos, and in the outer ring are
the huts of the married couples—described by Malinowski (1935, pp.430–
434) as the 'profane' part of the village. Thus there are important

structures or patterns in the plan—the opposition of sacred and profane space, and of centre and periphery; raw food is stored in the inner ring and no cooking is allowed there but must be done in the outer rings; only bachelors may live in the inner ring, while the married couples live in the outer ring. The spatial organisation of the village has in fact been made unselfconsciously to correspond with a whole variety of social beliefs and practices; each member of the culture is aware of the significance of the various spatial elements of the village and responds to them accordingly.

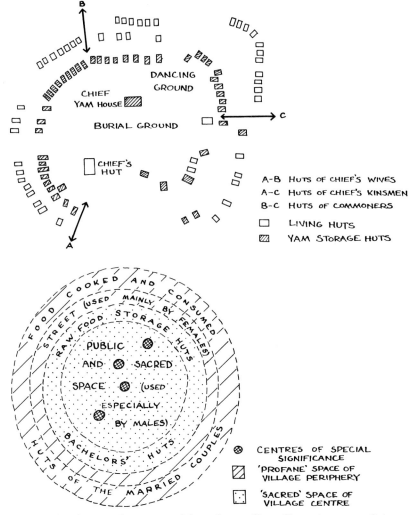

Figure 2.1. The spatial structure of Omarakama village, illustrating some of the structural features of the 'lived' or 'existential' space of the Trobriand Islanders (in part from Malinowski, 1935, p.25).

In other words, this existential space is both experienced and created unselfconsciously, that is without deliberate reflection or a prearranged plan, and in the context of the complete range of significances of the various spatial elements.

Because such existential space is meaningful within one culture group does not mean that it is communicable to members of other cultures, at least not without some considerable effort of understanding on their part.

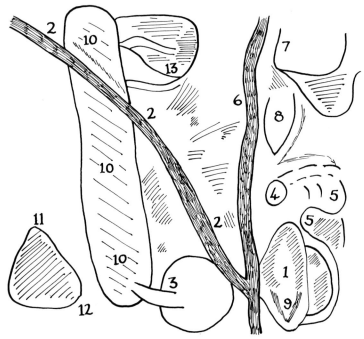

Figure 2.2. An Aboriginal map of the Gurudjmug Area (from Berndt and Berndt, 1970, p.56).

Key: 1. Gabari Creek.
  2. Gabari Waterhole.
  3. Gunyiguyimi Waterhole.
  4. A *njalaidj* ceremony was held close to (2); here people were dancing.
  5. People from the north who came to the *njalaidj* ceremony now stand here as rocks.
  6. Namalaid, an orphan was here.
  7. The orphan's elder brother went up here and was turned into a rock.
  8. Fishing net used by the fishermen who came to the *njalaidj*.
  9. The elder brother's dog.
  10. Nabamuli Billabong.
  11. Gurudjmug Hill.
  12. Galawan Goanna *djang* is at the top of this hill.
  13. Paperbark trees, now *djang*, left by the drowned people.
(*Djang*—spirit-being associated with specific site or place; *njalaidj*—a ceremony with trading.)

Consider for example Rapoport's account (1972, p.3-3-4) of the way in
which aborigines and Europeans see the landscape of north-west Australia:

"Many Europeans have spoken of the uniformity and featurelessness of
the Australian landscape. The aborigines, however, see the landscape in
a totally different way. Every feature of the landscape is known and
has meaning—they then perceive differences which the European cannot
see. These differences may be in terms of detail or in terms of a
magical and invisible landscape, the symbolic landscape being even more
varied than the perceived physical space. As one example, every
individual feature of Ayer's Rock is linked to a significant myth and the
mythological beings who created it. Every tree, every stain, hole and
fissure has meaning. Thus what to a European is an empty land may
be full of noticeable differences to the aborigines and hence rich and
complex."

This example is of interest not only because it shows that existential space
is culturally defined and hence it is difficult to experience the space of
another culture, but also because it indicates some ways in which the
space of a 'primitive' culture differs from that of Europeans. Thus
Rapoport notes that while Europeans—and indeed the members of all
modern technological societies—possess space by building and organise it
mainly in terms of material objects and functions, for the aborigines it is
structured according to places of myth, ceremony, and ritual, and is
everywhere peopled by spirit-beings. Space is full with significance, and
the landscape, rather than being comprised of physical and geological
features, is a record of mythical history in which the rocks and trees for
us are experienced as ancestors and spirits by the aborigines (figure 2.2).
There is in fact a very clear distinction to be drawn between the existential
space of a culture like that of the aborigines and most technological and
industrial cultures—the former is 'sacred' and symbolic, while the latter are
'geographical' and significant mainly for functional and utilitarian purposes.

2.3.1 Sacred space
Sacred space is that of archaic religious experience; it is continuously
differentiated and replete with symbols, sacred centres and meaningful
objects. For the religious person the experience of such space is primordial,
equivalent perhaps to an experience of the founding of the world, and it
follows that the making of sacred objects and sacred buildings (and in
some cultures that includes virtually all buildings) is not a task to be
undertaken lightly but involves a profound and total commitment.
Mircea Eliade (1959, p.11) believes that sacred experience involves the
"manifestation of something of a wholly different order, something that
does not belong to our world". Such experience obviously has profound
existential significance—above all it provides orientation by reference to
holy or sacred places. Sacred places are centres of the world—points at

which the three cosmic planes of heaven, earth, and hell are in contact and where communication between them is possible. Such centres are in no way to be understood as geometric, and indeed there may be an infinite number of sacred centres in any region all of which are considered, and even literally called, 'the centre of the world' (Eliade, 1961, p.39). Thus each temple, each palace, each hallowed area, and even each house insofar as it is itself a temple (Raglan, 1964), constitutes a sacred place.

Eliade (1959, p.24) suggests that sacred experience has been largely replaced by profane experience in modern societies: such profane experience gives spaces "that are not sacred and so without structure or consistency", though he qualifies this by observing that profane experiences are rarely found in a pure state. Nevertheless in comparison with the profound revelations and orientations that are given by the experience of space as sacred, these are only "fragments of a shattered universe".

2.3.2 Geographical space

Since in modern society desacralisation is pervasive, and truly sacred experience of the world is improbable if not impossible for most people, the 'fragments' assume considerable importance. They constitute the bases for what Eric Dardel (1952, p.2) terms 'geographical space'[3]: "Plain or mountain, ocean or equatorial forest, geographical space is made up of differentiated space ... . Geographical space is unique; it has its own name—Paris, Champagne, the Sahara, the Mediterranean". Geographical space is a reflection of man's basic awareness of the world, his experiences and intentional links with his environment. It is the significant space of a particular culture that is humanised by the naming of places, by its qualities for men, and by remaking it to serve better the needs of mankind.

Space is claimed for man by naming it. Jacquetta Hawkes (1951, p.151) writes: "Place names are among the things that link men most intimately with their territory" and suggests that since Palaeolithic times peopled landscapes have never been without some name to enrich and confirm their personality. The naming of regions and places is indeed part of a fundamental structuring of existential space. Irving Hallowell (1955, p.186) has stated: "Place naming, star naming, maps, myth and tale, the orientations of building, the spatial implications in dances and ceremonies,

---

[3] Several qualifications are needed here. First, Eliade clearly judges sacred space as more desirable than profane space. I do not wish to make such a judgement but merely to draw the distinction between the sacred and non-sacred experiences of space. Secondly, since the term 'profane' implies judgement I prefer to use Dardel's term 'geographical' to describe the non-sacred experience. Such experience is not necessarily shallow and may, if approached with openness, have very profound ontological significance [see the discussion of Heidegger's ideas in Vycinas (1961)]. Thirdly, the use of the term 'geographical space' must be understood in the context of the phenomenological basis of geography. For most professional geographers 'geographical space' means two-dimensional, cognitive, map space.

all facilitate the construction and maintenance of spatial patterns in which the individual must live and act". Where there are no names the environment is chaotic, lacking in orientation, even fearful, for it has no humanised and familiar points of reference. Thus when the Masai of Kenya were forced to relocate they took with them the names of hills, rivers and plains and fitted them to the new topography; similarly North America is sprinkled with the borrowed place names of Europe, for these once provided familiarity in an otherwise strange land (Lynch, 1972, p.41). Indeed one of man's first acts on entering any unexplored or uninhabited region is to give names to at least the most prominent features and thus to humanise the wilderness.

Geographical space is not objective and indifferent but full of significance for people. Dardel (1952, p.12) suggests that it appears as "essentially qualified in a concrete situation which affects man"—it has colour, depth, density, and solidity, it has associations and symbols, it both offers possibilities for and yet restricts experience. It is not an indifferent space that can be arranged or dismissed, but always has meaning in terms of some human task or lived-experience. Thus a prairie is 'vast', a mountain 'impassable', a house 'spacious' or a street 'constricted' only with reference to a particular human intention. But of course such things as prairies or houses are not experienced in some isolated way—intentionality merely gives direction to experience and the actual experiences are composed of whole complexes of visual, auditory and olfactory sensations, present circumstances and purposes, past experiences and associations, the unfolding sequence of vistas and the various cultural and aesthetic criteria by which we judge buildings and landscapes. For a farmer the space of the countryside is primarily the extent of his farm, the view across his fields, the way to the market—all experienced as enduring yet seasonally changing complexes. Such space, such landscape is not something just to be looked at, but is "for the insertion of man into the world, a place of combat for life" (Dardel, 1952, p.44). For the city-dweller the space of the city is only spread-out and extensive on those rare occasions when he looks down on it from some vantage point. More commonly his experience of cities is that of his home, his place of work, and the space of the street in all its variety of views, sounds and smells: "The town as geographical reality is the street—the street as the centre and realm of everyday life" (Dardel, 1952, p.37; see also Rudofsky, 1969).

The geographical space of countryside and town involves a close association between the experience and the creation of space. Landscape and townscape surround yet express human intention and presence for they are man-made or built. Building, suggests Heidegger (Vycinas, 1961, pp.14–15), is dwelling; dwelling is the essence of existence, the very manner by which men and women are on the earth, and involves an openness to and acceptance of the earth, the sky, the gods and our mortality [4]. In building which embraces dwelling there is no deliberate or selfconscious attempt to mould space as though it is an object—rather space is moulded, created, and possessed by the very act of building or landscape modification. The result is places which evolve, and have an organic quality, which have what Heidegger calls the character of 'sparing'—the tolerance of something for itself without trying to change it or control it—places which are evidence of care and concern for the earth and for other men. Such spaces and places are full with meaning; they have an order and a sense that can be experienced directly, yet which is infinitely variable.

When the fusion of dwelling and building, of the earth and the sky and the gods and mortals, is total, then geographical space is essentially sacred. It is tempting to identify this with the space of nonliterate and vernacular cultures where unselfconscious and traditional design and building procedures exist. Thus Eliade (1961, p.39) writes of such space: "What we have here is a sacred, mythic geography, the only kind effectually *real*, as opposed to profane geography, the latter being 'objective' and as it were abstract and non-essential—the theoretical construction of a space and a world that we do not live in, and therefore do not *know*." But this is too easy, a too simple dismissal of significant experience in industrial cultures and selfconscious space-making. Even the most uniform and 'care-lessly' planned spaces of contemporary urban development are named and structured into distinctive centres and districts. And even in deepest suburbia people put down roots and develop a concern for where they live (Taylor, 1973). Such experience is clearly not the same as that of the peasant in his home in the Black Forest described by Heidegger (Vycinas, 1961, p.16 and p.261), and it cannot have the equivalent intensity and depth of architectural expression, if only because the houses are built by subcontractors working from designs in pattern books. But at the same time we cannot easily judge it as a lesser experience, for it still involves the intentions, the hopes and fears of men and women. Of experience, as of happiness and despair, we have no measure (Haag, 1962, p.199).

2.3.3 Structure of geographical space

Some aspects of the structure of geographical space are well illustrated in studies of townscape like those by Gordon Cullen (1971) and Kevin Lynch (1960). Cullen analyses the experiences we have of urban space from the perspective of the person in the street, and seeks to establish the fundamental components of that experience, noting particularly the importance of serial vision, of places or centres, and of the content of those places (figure 2.3A). Lynch examines the images or mental pictures

[4] It is impossible to do justice to Heidegger's thought here, even though his writings are possibly the most relevant and the most significant on ontological foundations of place, space, building, and world. Furthermore any attempt at summary is unnecessary since an excellent introduction to these themes in Heidegger's work is available in Vycinas, *Earth and Gods* (1961).

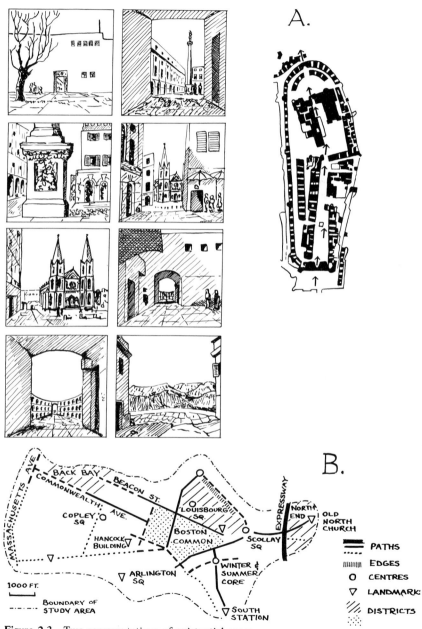

Figure 2.3. Two representations of existential space.
(A) Existential space as experienced in serial vision and from the perspective of the person in the street (from Cullen, 1971, p.17).
(B) The Boston image derived from street interviews. Existential space of the city analysed, aggregated, and mapped (from Lynch, 1960, p.153).

people have of cities, assuming that these are to a very great extent a
function of their experiences, and tries to determine the features of the
townscape that figure most prominently in those images (figure 2.3B).
Perhaps neither of these approaches indicates precisely what existential
urban space comprises—the former is too visual, and the latter is biased
by being aggregated and mapped into the cognitive space of formal street
plans—but together they characterise some of the more significant elements
of such space, and they do suggest some of its structural components.

Norberg-Schulz (1971, chapter 2) gives a more formal analysis of the
structuring of existential space, and identifies both a vertical and a
horizontal structure—basing the latter very much on Lynch's analysis.
First he identifies several levels of existential space (figure 2.4A). The
widest and most comprehensive of these is that of 'geography'—the level
at which meaning is given to nations, continents, and regions beyond our
direct experience (it therefore has a cognitive character). The next level
is that of landscape, the background to man's actions and a reflection of
his interactions with environment on a major scale. Below this is an
urban level, differing from that of landscape in that it is almost entirely
a built space created through human effort and purpose. The next level
is that of the street, the basis of our experience of cities; and below that
is the house, or more precisely the home, the central reference point of
human existence; "our home is our corner of the world ... it is our first
universe, a real cosmos in every sense of the word" (Bachelard, 1969, p.4).
Of all levels of existential space this is perhaps the most fundamental, for,
as Bachelard (1969, p.5) points out, "all really inhabited space bears the
essence of the notion of home". Finally there is the level of the object—
a material space in which the value of objects is determined by their
significance as utensils, or a symbolic space in which the objects or things
represent other spaces and experiences.

This structure reflects both a change in scale from the largest to the
smallest extent and an increasing humanisation of space. Such a structure
is not, of course, explicit in all our experiences, and the levels need not
always be of exactly the form presented here. But in general it seems
that we do live in terms of a variety of levels though at any one moment
our attention is focused on just one level: in voting our concern is with
national space, but in finding the polling booth it is the spaces of the city
and street that are important.

At each of these levels there is a more or less clearly identifiable
horizontal structure (figure 2.4B). This comprises three major elements.
First there is a set of *districts* or regions of particular significance, defined
by the interests and experiences of the groups concerned: "these various
realms of relevances are intermingled, showing the most manifold
interpenetrations and enclaves", they are not clear-cut, disparate regions
(Schütz, 1962, Vol.2, p.126). These are organised and opened up by *paths* or

routes which reflect the directions and intensities of intentions and
experiences, and which serve as the structural axes of existential space.
They radiate from and lead towards nodes or centres of special importance
and meaning which are distinguished by their quality of insideness. These
are *places*. This pattern of places, paths and districts is repeated in some

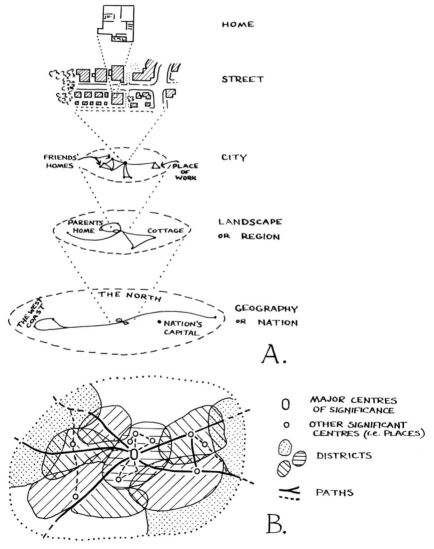

Figure 2.4. Vertical and horizontal structures of existential space.
(A) Levels of the vertical structure, especially as they apply to urban spaces (based on
   an analysis by Norberg-Schulz, 1971).
(B) Components of the horizontal structure of existential space.

form at all the levels of existential space. Sometimes it corresponds
directly to the physical features of the landscape—roads, buildings, vistas
(figure 2.3B); sometimes it corresponds to mythical phenomena, such as
paths to heaven and hell or the sites of mythical events (figure 2.2 and
figure 2.6B); and sometimes it reflects particular intentions or biases, such
as an architect's concern with buildings. In short, the structure has no
fixed orientation or scale, but reflects the interests and concerns of the
cultural group of which it is an expression.

Places in existential space can therefore be understood as centres of
meaning, or focuses of intention and purpose. The types of meanings and
functions defining places need not be the same for all cultural groups, nor
do the centres have to be clearly demarcated by physical features, but
they must have an inside that can be experienced as something differing
from an outside. For many religious peoples places are holy and within
the context of a powerful symbolic and sacred space. For the contemporary
European or North American most places have a much weaker symbolic
content than this, and are defined largely by the meanings or significant
associations attached to buildings, landforms, or areas in specific locations.
But in both cases places constitute significant centres of experience within
the context of the lived-space of the everyday social world.

2.4 Architectural space and planning space
Existential space combines an experience of space with a remaking of the
spaces of the lived-world, and both these activities are largely without
formal conceptualisation. In contrast, architectural space, although founded
on and contributing to unselfconscious spatial experiences, involves a
deliberate attempt to create spaces (Norberg-Schulz, 1971, pp.13–16).
The space of city planning, however, is not based on experiences of space,
but is concerned primarily with function in two-dimensional map space.

Siegfried Giedion (1963) has identified three major manifestations of
architectural space—each corresponding to a phase of architectural
development. The first of these is the space created by an interplay
between volumes, and this was associated especially with the buildings of
the Greek and Egyptian civilisations; thus Greek temples defined space
largely in terms of the relationship between them. The second form of
space is that of hollowed-out interior space, and this was manifest in a
style that dated from the building of the Pantheon to the late 18th
century and was apparent not only in temple and church interiors but also
in such external features as Renaissance plazas. The third form is the
treatment of space from several perspectives simultaneously, involving the
free manipulation of the relationships between inside and outside that
characterises much contemporary architecture. The implications of this
classification for the present discussion have been expressed well by
Gauldie (1969, p.78). He notes that while architectural space has a

variety of expressions, these are all initially concerned with the imaginative experience of space; the ability to create architectural space which encourages such experiences is very dependent on individual genius, but the possibility of achieving them appears to be greatest where abstract ideas of space are most highly developed.

The space of urban planning is well linked to architectural space— indeed in the Renaissance they were essentially the same and there was a resulting continuity between buildings and streets and squares. More recently architectural space has come to be that of individual buildings conceived and constructed in isolation. In comparison to the attention lavished on these individual structures the nature and experience of the spaces between buildings has been left largely to chance, resulting in what Brett (1970, p.117) has termed SLOIP, an appropriately awful acronym for Space Left Over in Planning. Planning for the *experience* of total urban space has been meagre indeed, and the space of modern urban planning is primarily the two-dimensional, cognitive space of maps and plans. This is obvious in the widespread use of grids and curvilinear street patterns, in the careful separation of function categories of land-use, in the casual laying-down of transportation networks. Space is understood to be empty and undifferentiated and objectively manipulable according to the constraints of functional efficiency, economics, and the whims of planners and developers. Thus Wingo (1963, p.7) describes space as a resource to meet future growth requirements, and suggests that the main problem it presents is how to structure most efficiently the social and economic activities to be located. In short, planning space does not involve direct or imaginative experience but order on maps and land-use efficiency.

This may be overstressing the differences between planning and architectural space. There is, of course, a functional architectural tradition in which little attention has been paid to the experience of the spaces of buildings in any sense—reflecting perhaps the assertion of Gropius that "architecture is the mastery of space" (cited in Brett, 1970, p.46). But that there is nevertheless a significant difference in the attitude of architects and planners is particularly apparent in their discussions and use of the notion of place. The essential task of the architect, Sinclair Gauldie maintains (1969, p.173), is "the creation of place in the sense that he has to set about endowing some considerable part of the human environment with a new and special order". Susanne Langer (1953, pp.93–96) adopts a similar line of thought, suggesting that architects deal with created space and that this is something quite imaginary or conceptual which has been translated into visual and other impressions. Within the context of created spaces she finds the basic abstraction of architecture is the 'ethnic domain', that is, "a place made visible, tangible, sensible". To illustrate what she means by this she gives the example of a gypsy camp: "Literally we say the camp is *in* a place; culturally it *is* a place", and has its own functional realm and its own symbolic properties; it is in effect both the centre of and a symbol for the whole world. The architect's task is thus to express this cultural and symbolic complex of the ethnic domain, and to achieve selfconsciously and deliberately the creation of significant places within the context of existential space.

There have been selfconscious attempts to capitalise on the idea of place, and Jencks (1973, pp.302–328) suggests that there is something akin to a 'place' movement in modern architecture, in which a deliberate effort is made to capture 'multi-meaning', to provide a sense of the identity and reality of place. Of course this is one among many and diverse approaches in contemporary architecture but it is important to recognise that whatever principles or theories or concepts the architect works with the created building will inevitably be experienced in some way by its users or its viewers as a place, as a centre of human associations and significances.

The concept of place used in planning is quite different from this; in planning it means little more than a location where certain specified interactions occur and certain limited functions are served. It is a shopping centre or service centre of a suburban neighbourhood or an arbitrarily defined community that can be identified on a map. This is a notion of place that clearly owes little to spatial experience but is closely tied to cognitive space.

2.5 Cognitive space

Cognitive space consists of the abstract construct of space derived from the identification of space as an object for reflection and the attempt to develop theories about it. Einstein has suggested (Jammer, 1969, p.xiii) that "the concept of space ... was preceded by the psychologically simpler concept of place", and indeed in western civilisation the first really coherent statements about place, notably Aristotle's theory of place, were the first tentative approaches to a conceptualisation of space. Thus Archytas (cited in Jammer, 1969, p.10) argued that "every body occupies some place, and cannot exist unless its place exists. Since what is moved is moved into a certain place and doing and suffering are motions, it is plain that place, in which what is done and suffered exists, is the first of things." Aristotle's theory was essentially an extension of this argument. He maintained that while the place of a thing is no part of it, and a place and a thing can be separated, a place is defined by "the boundary of that which encloses it", and is "wherever a material object is, or it is logically possible could be" (W. K. C. Guthrie, cited in Lukermann, 1961, p.207; Swinburne, 1968, p.12). The essence of this concept lies in the relative location of things, and this is preserved and made systematic in Euclidean space, where place is basically understood as location definable by sets of coordinates. Cognitive space is a homogeneous space, with equal value everywhere and in all directions. It is uniform and it is neutral, a dimension, the space of geometry and maps and theories of spatial organisation (figure 2.5). It is a form of space that is reflected on, and which would have little significance for direct experience were it not for the fact that geometries and maps and theories are not infrequently the bases of plans and designs.

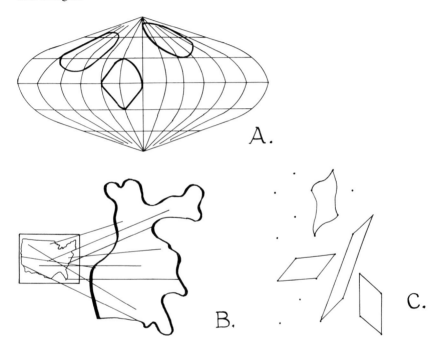

Figure 2.5. Some forms of cognitive and abstract space.
(A) A sinusoidal map projection—the distorted figures are true circles on the surface of the earth (from Patton et al., 1970, p.26). Map projections are perhaps the clearest expression of cognitive space.
(B) A topological transformation of the map of the United States—a transformation of cognitive into abstract space (from Bunge, 1962, p.221).
(C) Examples of fundamental regions—areas in the plane of a lattice that will fill exactly the entire lattice by using just the X and Y translations that generated the original lattice points to transport the area over the plane (from Bunge, 1962, p.226).

2.6 Abstract space
The distinction between abstract and cognitive space is one that has only recently been identified, coming perhaps with the recognition that Euclidean space is not necessarily a faithful reflection of some absolute space, but is simply a human construct, and that other geometries and topologies are not only possible but might even be more accurate in some circumstances (Norberg-Schulz, 1971, p.10; Hawkins, 1964, chapter 2).

Abstract space is the space of logical relations that allows us to describe space without necessarily founding those descriptions in empirical observations (figure 2.5). It is a free creation of the human imagination and as such is a direct reflection of the achievement of symbolic thought. "We must admit that abstract space has no counterpart and no foundation in physical or psychological reality", Ernst Cassirer has declared (1970, pp.48–49). "The points and lines of the geometer are neither physical nor psychological objects; they are nothing but symbols for abstract relations". In abstract space all the concrete differences of our sense experiences are eliminated; space is conceived, for example, as "continuous, isotropic, homogeneous, finite or infinite" (Jammer, 1969, p.7). In such space places are merely points, symbols constituting just one element within the overall system of abstract elements.

2.7 Relationships between the forms of space
This classification of forms of consciousness of space reveals a wide range of meanings for space as well as a variety of significances for place. It is, of course, not the only classification possible; Jeanne Hersch (cited in Matoré, 1962, pp.113–114) distinguishes transcendental, practical, social, physical and mathematical space (cf Dardel, 1952; Tuan, 1975). Nor are the types of space to be understood as clearly separated. On the contrary, they are closely linked both in thought and experience. Norberg-Schulz (1971, p.11) suggests that "pragmatic space integrates man with his natural, 'organic' environment, perceptual space is essential to his identity as a person, existential space makes him belong to a social and cultural totality, cognitive space means he is able to think about space, and logical space ... offers him a tool to describe the others". To these can be added the built and planned spaces that integrate experience and thought. All this may suggest some sort of progression from pragmatic to abstract space, but this is inaccurate for in present-day technical cultures cognitive notions everywhere influence our experience and creation of spaces. Knowledge of maps and plans is a fundamental part of our experiences of existential and perceptual space—thus we use road and street maps to find our way around not only cities that are unfamiliar but also the cities and towns we live in, and a prominent image for any region or urban area is its map shape. And cognitive ideas serve both selfconsciously and unselfconsciously as the bases for creating almost all the environments in which we live; even 'natural, organic space' is for most people founded in the planned spaces of cities or of surveyed and geometric countrysides.

Place, in association with space, also has a multiplicity of interrelated meanings. Place is not a simple undifferentiated phenomenon of experience that is constant in all situations, but instead has a range of subtleties and significances as great as the range of human experiences and intentions. Thus Aldo van Eyck (1969, p.209) writes that "a village

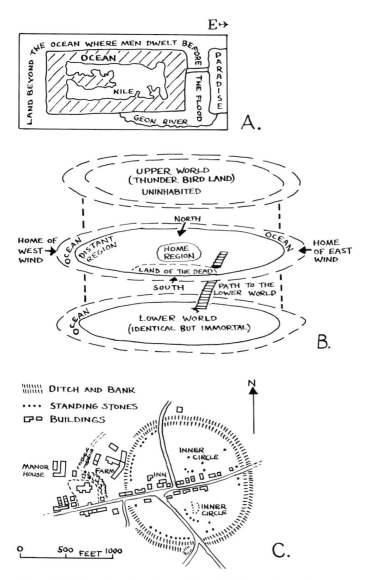

Figure 2.6. Examples of an intermixing of different forms of space.

(A) The world according to the Christian topographer Cosmas. In his scheme are combined primitive notions of cognitive space and elements of sacred space.

(B) Cosmographic notions of the Salteaux Indians (based on an account by Hallowell, 1955). This combines existential space and sacred space with ideas of cognitive and perhaps elements of pragmatic space.

(C) The village of Avebury in Wiltshire, England, partly sited within a neolithic stone circle. Here are 'dead' sacred space and the unselfconsciously created space of the village, both expressed in the cognitive space of a map.

(town or city) is not just one bunch of places; it is many bunches at the same time, because it is a different bunch for each inhabitant ...". For a Bostonian answering questions about the significant elements of the city's identity the distinctive places are the obvious tourist features: Boston Common, the Old North Church, Paul Revere's House; but for a Bostonian going about his daily routine the significant places are his home and his place of work. There is no contradiction in this—in fact the personal places of the direct experiences of perceptual space are organised in the context of and provide the basis of the more public places of existential space. And both of these are in turn known within the framework of the formally located places of cognitive space. That what we know as places changes as our intentions shift should not be considered a source of confusion, rather it is a source of richness in our geographical experience with each type of place complementing the others.

Those aspects of space that we distinguish as places are differentiated because they have attracted and concentrated our intentions, and because of this focusing they are set apart from the surrounding space while remaining a part of it. But the meaning of space, and particularly lived-space, comes from the existential and perceptual places of immediate experience. This meaning and this relationship are profound; Heidegger (cited in Norberg-Schulz, 1971, p.16) has written: "Spaces receive their being from places and not from 'the space' ... . Man's essential relationship to places, and through them to space, consists in dwelling ... the essential property of human existence."

3

The essence of place

In our everyday lives places are not experienced as independent, clearly defined entities that can be described simply in terms of their location or appearance. Rather they are sensed in a chiaroscuro of setting, landscape, ritual, routine, other people, personal experiences, care and concern for home, and in the context of other places. It is therefore essential to attend carefully to John Donat's caution (1967, p.9) about attempting to understand places: "Places occur at all levels of identity, my place, your place, street, community, town, county, region, country and continent, but places never conform to tidy hierarchies of classification. They all overlap and interpenetrate one another and are wide open to a variety of interpretation." But while complexity and variety of scale may well be desirable qualities in terms of our experiences of places, when it comes to trying to understand place as a phenomenon these same qualities present major stumbling blocks. There is, however, one possibility for clarifying place. By taking place as a multifaceted phenomenon of experience and examining the various properties of place, such as location, landscape, and personal involvement, some assessment can be made of the degree to which these are essential to our experience and sense of place. In this way the sources of meaning, or essence of place can be revealed.

3.1 Place and location
In describing his first voyage to Latin America Lévi-Strauss (1971, p.66) wrote: "It was the opposite of 'travel', in that the ship seemed to us not so much a means of transport as a place of residence—a home, in fact, before which Nature put on a new show every morning." This is a theme that is explored in a more philosophical way by Susanne Langer (1953, p.95) in her account of the idea of place in architecture. She argues that places are culturally defined and that location in the strict cartographic sense is merely an incidental quality of place:

> "... A ship constantly changing its location is nonetheless a selfcontained place, and so is a gypsy camp, an Indian camp, or a circus camp, however often it shifts its geodetic bearings. Literally we say a camp is *in* a place, but culturally it *is* a place. A gypsy camp is a different place from an Indian camp though it may be geographically where the Indian camp used to be."

These are, of course, somewhat exceptional examples—most places are indeed located—but they do indicate that location or position is neither a necessary nor a sufficient condition of place, even if it is a very common condition. This is of considerable importance for it demonstrates that mobility or nomadism do not preclude an attachment to place—peoples such as the Bororo of Brazil may demolish their villages every three years and rebuild them elsewhere but still maintain close ties to the places where they live (Choay, 1969, p.29). Similarly in contemporary society the most mobile and transient people are not automatically homeless or placeless, but may be able to achieve very quickly an attachment to new places either because the landscapes are similar to ones already well-known or because those people are open to new experiences. Ian Nairn (1965, p.10) writes: "People put down roots ... in a terribly short time; I myself take about forty-eight hours ... I would even argue paradoxically, that that mobility increases the sense of place."

3.2 Place and landscape
Susanne Langer (1953, p.99) continues her discussion of architectural place by suggesting that:

> "... a 'place' articulated by the imprint of human life must seem organic, like a living form ... . The place which a house occupies on the face of the earth, that is to say, its location in actual space, remains the same place if the house burns up or is wrecked and removed. But the place created by the architect is illusion, begotten by the visible expression of feeling, sometimes called an 'atmosphere'. This kind of place disappears if the house is destroyed ... ."

Although this is a complex conception of place as possessing intangible qualities and changing through time, the suggestion is that, above all, place has a physical, visual form—a landscape. Certainly appearance, whether of buildings or natural features, is one of the most obvious attributes of place. It is substantial, capable of being described. As visual landscape place has its clearest articulation in distinct centres or prominent features such as walled towns, nucleated villages, hilltops or the confluence of rivers, and it is usually such clearly defined and publicly observable places that feature in travel accounts or in simple geographical descriptions. But place as landscape is not always so naively apparent. Lawrence Durrell (1969, p.157), in a partly serious caricature of environmental determinism, argues that human beings are expressions of their landscape and that their cultural productions always bear the unmistakable signature of place:

> "I believe you could exterminate the French at one blow and resettle the country with Tartars, and within two generations discover to your astonishment that the national characteristics were back at norm—the restless metaphysical curiosity, the tenderness for good living and the passionate individualism: even though their noses were flat. This is the invisible constant in a place."

In short, the spirit of a place lies in its landscape. In a similar, if less extreme, vein Rene Dubos (1972) suggests that there is a 'persistence of place'—or a continuity in the appearance and spirit of places; just as the individuality and distinctiveness of the appearance of any one person endures from childhood to old age, so the identity of a particular place can persist through many external changes because there is some inner, hidden force—'a god within'. Whether this rather mystical argument is appealing or not, the importance of particular associations of physical features, both natural or man-made, in defining place cannot be denied. Even Martin Heidegger (Vycinas, 1961) in his ontological discussions of place, home, and the relations between man, earth, the sky and the gods, puts considerable emphasis on the visual properties of landscape, using examples of bridges, a Greek temple, and a peasant's house in the Black Forest.

Whether place is understood and experienced as landscape in the direct and obvious sense that visual features provide tangible evidence of some concentration of human activities, or in a more subtle sense as reflecting human values and intentions, appearance is an important feature of all places. But it is hardly possible to understand all place experiences as landscape experiences. There is the common sensation of returning to a familiar place after an absence of several years and feeling that everything has changed even though there have been no important changes in its appearance. Whereas before we were involved in the scene, now we are an outsider, an observer, and can recapture the significance of the former place only by some act of memory.

3.3 Place and time

The changing character of places through time is of course related to modifications of buildings and landscapes as well as to changes in our attitudes, and is likely to seem quite dramatic after a prolonged absence. On the other hand, the persistence of the character of places is apparently related to a continuity both in our experience of change and in the very nature of change that serves to reinforce a sense of association and attachment to those places. The Royal Commission on Local Government in England and Wales, for example, found that people claimed that their attachment to their 'home area' increased with the length of the time they had lived there, and was generally strongest when they lived in the same area they were born in (cited in Hampton, 1970, p.112). The implication of this is presumably that, as the residents' attachment becomes more pronounced, their home area or place changes its character for them, both because of improving geographical and social knowledge and especially because of a growing intensity of involvement and commitment. The result of such a growing attachment, imbued as it is with a sense of continuity, is the feeling that this place has endured and will persist as a distinctive entity even though the world around may change.

This is misleading of course. The places identified by any individual or culture grow, flourish, and decline as the site, activity, or buildings take on and lose significance. There may be a progression of such significances with the present places growing out of and replacing earlier ones, in much the same way that Jericho was repeatedly built on the ruins of the previous city on that site, and each new city is both the same place and yet a different place from its predecessors. Some places have died—the world is indeed full of the skeletons of dead places, Stonehenge and Carnac, the ruined cities of the Aztecs and Incas, ghost towns, and abandoned farms, which have been stripped of their original meanings and become little more than objects of casual and uncommitted observation for tourists and passers-by and other outsiders. Such withering away and modification are prevented by ritual and tradition that reinforce the sense of permanence of place. Such rituals may be obvious—for instance, the 'beating of the bounds' in some areas of England in which there is an annual procession around the parish boundary, or the Roman *lustratio* in which the boundary lines of farms and possibly also of cities were made sacred by an annual boundary procession (Fowler, 1971, pp.212–214). These serve both to redefine the place symbolically and legally, and to make its bounds known to the children of that place. But almost any form of repetitive tradition reestablishes place and expresses its stability and continuity—even in times of violent change. Frances Fitzgerald (1974, p.16) writes of villagers in Vietnam, some of whom have moved their homes eighteen or more times in the last twenty years, whose villages have been bombed and shelled and eventually bulldozed:

> "Where do the villagers' reserves of energy come from? From my visits to the liberated zones it seemed to me that it had to do with a certain view of history ... . Their dimension was time, not space ... . Just before we left his home the patriarch ... explained to us why he insisted that we, strangers and foreigners, should come to share his ancestral feast. "Your visit", he said, "was propitious. The foreigners destroyed our houses, our fields, and the tombs of our ancestors, and today you come to celebrate the anniversary of our ancestors. It is a good omen for peace." In one sentence of welcome he had managed to bracket thirty years of war and reduce it to an insignificant period within the history of his family. Such a perspective clearly did not admit of despair for within it the present could not be endless."

Such involvement with place is founded on the easy grasping of time spans of centuries, particularly by the persistence of tradition and through ancestor worship. A Vietnamese woman farming in the middle of what amounted to a battlefield explained simply—"But this is the land of my ancestors, so I couldn't leave" (Fitzgerald, 1974, p.14).

Much ritual and custom and myth has the incidental if not deliberate effect of strengthening attachment to place by reaffirming not only the sanctity and unchanging significance of it, but also the enduring relationships between a people and their place. When the rituals and myths lose their significance and the people cease to participate fully in them the places themselves become changeable and ephemeral. In cultures such as our own, where significant tradition counts for little, places may be virtually without time, except perhaps in terms of direct and personal experience. This does not mean just that there is no awareness of history, but also, and more profoundly, that places can become almost independent of time. This is the theme of Thomas Mann's novel *The Magic Mountain* (n.d., p.105):

> "Our first days in a new place time has a youthful, that is to say, a broad and sweeping flow ... . Then, as one 'gets used to the place' a gradual shrinkage makes itself felt. He who clings to, or better expressed, wishes to cling to life, will shudder to see how the days grow light and lighter, how they scurry by like dead leaves ..."

There is only routine, changes in appearance and activity lose any significance, tradition never was important, and place becomes a scarcely changing, overwhelming present. Time is usually a part of our experiences of places, for these experiences must be bound up with flux or continuity. And places themselves are the present expressions of past experiences and events and of hopes for the future. But, as Thomas Mann indicated, the essence of place does not lie either in timelessness or in continuity through time. These are simply dimensions, albeit important and unavoidable ones, that affect our experiences of place.

3.4 Place and community
The Royal Commission on Local Government in England concluded that while attachment to 'home area' increased with length of residence in that area, such attachment is primarily "concerned with the interaction of the individual with other people—rather than with his relationship to his physical environment" (cited in Hampton, 1970, p.115). In other words the Commission subscribed to the not uncommon view that a place is essentially its people and that appearance or landscape are little more than a backdrop of relatively trivial importance. Thus Alvin Toffler (1970, pp.91–94) suggests that in present-day western society many people feel at home wherever they are with people of similar interests, regardless of the particular place they are in. Such an emphasis on community seems to be an overly extreme denial of the importance of physical setting in place experience, if only for the simple reasons proposed by Minar and Greer (1969, p.47) that "the human contacts on which feelings of commitment and identity are built are most likely to occur among people sharing the same piece of ground". And the fact that we do not attend continually to our landscape and place does not make it insignificant, for in much the same way we usually take our own appearance, or that of our friends, very much for granted, even though it is a fundamental part of personal identity.

The relationship between community and place is indeed a very powerful one in which each reinforces the identity of the other, and in which the landscape is very much an expression of communally held beliefs and values and of interpersonal involvements. Thus the Mbuti pygmies of the Congo organise their village camp and the orientation of the doorways of the huts according to current friendships and animosities and the village and house plans are flexible and direct expressions of the social relationships in the community (Turnbull, 1965, p.357). In our own geography such flexibility is not possible, but social divisions are nevertheless often apparent in the different landscapes of the affluent, the bourgeoisie, and the poor, and through residents' and ratepayers' groups many people identify sufficiently with their local areas to attempt to protect them against change and development. In some form such relationships between created place and community exist in all cultures for reasons well summarised by Wagner (1972, p.53):

> "Communal undertakings bring together the families of a place for common ends: to apportion lands among families, provide water and other utilities, make and maintain roads, erect public buildings, create burial grounds, establish shrines and places of worship. The settlement lives in communal efforts despite the several separatenesses it harbours. And the acknowledged common fate and identity have their own expression in symbols and other display."

In particular they are expressed in the landscape, which in this sense is a medium of communication in which all the elements may have messages— buildings, streets, parades, village soccer teams, all serve not only to unite communities but also to make them explicit. And the commonly experienced messages and symbols of the landscape then serve to maintain what Aldo van Eyck (1969, p.109) has appropriately called "a collectively conditioned place consciousness", and this gives the people from a place essentially the same identity that the place itself has, and vice versa. Ronald Blythe (1969, pp.17–18) touches on this in his sensitive study of the village of Akenfield in East Anglia:

> "The villager who has never moved away from his birthplace ... retains the unique mark of his particular village. If a man says he comes from Akenfield he knows that he is telling someone from another part of the neighbourhood a good deal more than this. Anything from his appearance to his politics could be involved."

In short, people are their place and a place is its people, and however readily these may be separated in conceptual terms, in experience they are not easily differentiated. In this context places are 'public'—they are created and known through common experiences and involvement in common symbols and meanings.

There is another type of public place—one which is not to be understood primarily in terms of community but by its physical or symbolic qualities of 'placeness'. Thus enclaves and enclosures, city squares, walled towns and nucleated villages offer a distinctive experience of being inside, of being in a place (Cullen, 1971, pp.21–36). Similarly crossroads, central points or focuses, landmarks whether natural or man-made, tend not only to draw attention to themselves but also to declare themselves as places that in some way stand out from the surrounding area. Because of their centrality or clarity of form, remarkable size, exceptional architecture, or unusual natural features, or because of their associations with events of great significance, such as the birth or death of heroes, battles, or the signing of treaties, such places possess "high imageability" (Lynch, 1960). Imageability is not a fixed or absolute feature and the significant places of former times may be overwhelmed by larger forms or lose their significance, much as the church spires of medieval towns were lost among the factory chimneys of the nineteenth century and both were dwarfed by the skyscrapers of the twentieth century. But public places with high imageability do nevertheless tend to persist and to form an ongoing focus for common experience—Red Square in Moscow, Niagara Falls, the Acropolis, have all attracted public attention through many changes in fashion and political systems and beliefs.

Public places which achieve their publicity through high imageability are not necessary innocent—their distinctive appearance or form may be capitalised upon or even created as a statement of grandeur and authority to be regarded in awe by the common people. Lewis Mumford (1961, pp.386–391) has observed that the city planning and monumental architecture of the Renaissance and especially of the Baroque period was frequently an expression of secular and military power carried out by military engineers at the command of the local ruler. Similarly all royal palaces, the vast squares of the Third Reich, the monumental buildings of Stalinist Russia, the great avenues of Washington, left or leave little doubt as to where the centre of power lay and who wielded it. More recently the grandest and hugest buildings have been those of giant corporations— the high-rise office buildings significantly located in city centres, designed by the most famous architects, named after the principal developer (U.S. Steel in Pittsburgh, John Hancock in Boston, Shell in London, Toronto Dominion in Toronto) and always competing to be the highest. But whether the builder is a monarch, a dictator, or a giant corporation, there are Machiavellian intentions involved in all such public place-making that have been summarised by Robert Goodman (1971, p.103): "The more magnificent and monumental the official public places the more trivial becomes the citizen's personal environment, and the more he tends to be awed by the official environment ...". It is in and through these official public places that centralised governments and organisations make overt their status and authority—and pageants and parades such as the May Day

Parade in Red Square, or the Pope's blessing of the crowd in St. Peter's Square serve always to reinforce the authoritative significance of these places.

Official public places are not all so obviously expressed. Indeed film and television, which reduce the scale of such building and cannot adequately convey the experience of architectural domination, may have made massiveness as an element of public place-making anachronistic. The significant public places of power are now the steps of 10 Downing Street, the Front Lawn or Oval Office of the White House, and similar small discreet places. It is here that important decisions are announced, and statements made to the cameras and microphones and hence to the public, though paradoxically these places are often not directly accessible to that public.

3.5 Private and personal places

Official public places and those which are communally experienced are only particular forms of the phenomenon of place, and although common experience is unquestionably an important element in understanding place it does not suffice to define its essence. All places and landscapes are individually experienced, for we alone see them through the lens of *our* attitudes, experiences, and intentions, and from our own unique circumstances (Lowenthal, 1961). Indeed J.K.Wright (1947, pp.3–4) has suggested that "the entire earth is an immense patchwork of miniature *terrae incognitae*"—the private geographies of individuals. Important though it is to acknowledge this individual colouring of all landscapes, it is scarcely more than recognising that any landscape is experienced both individually and in a communal context, for we are all individuals and members of society.

Of more significance are those private places that are set apart from the public world either physically or because of their particular meaning for us. Richard Hoggart (1959, pp.32–38) notes that in English working-class culture the living-room/kitchen constitutes a deeply private place, and is truly the centre of both family and individual life. And within that one room each person may well have his or her own place—a special chair or group of objects. This seems to apply in rather different cultural situations—for instance in Forest Hill, one of the more affluent districts of Toronto, Seeley *et al.* (1956, p.56) observed that in the home there should be "... a desk or its equivalent in a well demarcated area for each member of the family 'old enough'. These areas may be rooms or merely corners, shelves or drawers ... . When occupying 'his' space the individual should not be disturbed; when absent his possessions are not to be rearranged ... ".

Clearly these physically defined and publicly respected places are important for each of us, for they are expressions of our individuality.

But private places need not be quite so immediate and obvious. There may indeed be no common knowledge of them; rather they are defined by special and particular significances for us, and may be remembered rather than immediately present. In particular the places of childhood constitute vital reference points for many individuals. They may be special locations and settings which serve to recall particular personal experiences, though the setting itself may be no part of that experience; thus Rene Dubos writes (1972, p.87): "I remember the mood of places better than their precise features because places evoke for me life situations rather than geographical sites." Or there may be personal places which in themselves are the source of some "peak experience" as Maslow (1968) has called it—that is, an ecstatic experience of pure individuality and identity that stems from some encounter with place. It is of such an experience that Wallace Stegner writes (1962, pp.21-22):

> "I still sometimes dream ... of a bend of the Whitemud River below Martin's Dam. Every time I have that dream I am haunted, on awaking, by a sense of meanings just withheld, and by a profound nostalgic melancholy ... . What interests me is the mere fact that this dead loop of a river, known only for a few years, should be so charged with potency in my consciousness ... this is still the place toward which my well-conditioned unconsciousness turns like an old horse heading for the barn."

In Stegner's case it is the dreamt and remembered place that provides the significant personal experience. But a direct experience of place can be equally profound, and whether it is an abrupt and ecstatic experience, or a slowly developed, gently grown involvement, what is important is the sense that *this* place is uniquely and privately your own because your experience of it is distinctively personal. Albert Camus (1959, p.70) wrote of his experience of the view from the Boboli Gardens at Florence: "Millions of eyes, I knew, had looked on this landscape and it was still, for me, the first smile of the sky. It put me outside myself in the most profound sense of the word". This is quite literally 'topophilia'—an encounter with place that is intensely personal and profoundly significant (Tuan, 1961, 1974).

3.6 Rootedness and care for place
In both our communal and our personal experience of places there is often a close attachment, a familiarity that is part of knowing and being known *here*, in this particular place. It is this attachment that constitutes our roots in places; and the familiarity that this involves is not just a detailed knowledge, but a sense of deep care and concern for that place.

To be attached to places and have profound ties with them is an
important human need. Simone Weil wrote in *The Need for Roots* (1955,
p.53):

> "To be rooted is perhaps the most important and least recognised need
> of the human soul. It is one of the hardest to define. A human
> being has roots by virtue of his real, active and natural participation in
> the life of the community, which preserves in living shape certain
> particular expectations for the future. This participation is a natural
> one in the sense that it is automatically brought about by place,
> conditions of birth, profession and social surroundings. Every human
> being needs to have multiple roots. It is necessary for him to draw
> well-nigh the whole of his moral, intellectual and spiritual life by way
> of the environment of which he forms a part."

The need for roots, Weil suggested by implication, is at least equivalent to
the need for order, liberty, responsibility, equality, and security—and
indeed to have roots in a place is perhaps a necessary precondition for the
other 'needs of the soul'. This is what Robert Coles is suggesting when he
writes at the conclusion of his study of uprooted children in the United
States (1970, pp.120–121):

> "It is utterly part of our nature to want roots, to need roots, to
> struggle for roots, for a sense of belonging, for some place that is
> recognised as *mine*, as *yours*, as *ours*. Nations, regions, states, counties,
> cities, towns—all of them have to do with politics and geography and
> history; but they are more than that, for they somehow reflect man's
> humanity, his need to stay someplace and get to know ... other people
> ... and what I suppose can be called a particular environment or space
> or neighbourhood or set of circumstances."

To have roots in a place is to have a secure point from which to look out
on the world, a firm grasp of one's own position in the order of things,
and a significant spiritual and psychological attachment to somewhere in
particular.

The places to which we are most attached are literally fields of care,
settings in which we have had a multiplicity of experiences and which call
forth an entire complex of affections and responses. But to care for a
place involves more than having a concern for it that is based on certain
past experiences and future expectations—there is also a real responsibility
and respect for that place both for itself and for what it is to yourself and
to others. There is, in fact, a complete commitment to that place, a
commitment that is as profound as any that a person can make, for care-
taking is indeed "the basis of man's relation to the world" (Vycinas, 1961,
p.33).

Such commitment and responsibility entails what Heidegger has called
'sparing' (Vycinas, 1961, p.266): sparing is letting things, or in this

context places, be the way they are; it is a tolerance for them in their own essence; it is taking care of them through building or cultivating without trying to subordinate them to human will. Sparing is a willingness to leave places alone and not to change them casually or arbitrarily, and not to exploit them. Care-taking and sparing are illustrated well in Heidegger's example of a peasant house in the Black Forest that respects the earth, the sky, the gods and men—for Heidegger the four essential facets of human existence (Vycinas, 1961, p.261):

> "There, when a man built his home near a spring and facing south on a hillside protected from the raw winds, it was the earth itself which directed the construction of such a building; and man by being open to the demands of the earth was merely a responder. When he extended the roof far down past the wall of the house and gave it sufficient slope, he had taken into consideration the stormy winter skies and possible accumulations of snow on the roof. Here too, the weather, or rather the sky, determined the structure of the building. A built-in corner for prayer was a response to God, and a place for a cradle and a coffin reflected man in his mortality."

It is only through this type of sparing and care-taking that 'home' can be properly realized, and to have a home is to 'dwell'—which is for Heidegger (1971) the essence of human existence and the basic character of Being.

3.7 Home places as profound centres of human existence

Vincent Vycinas (1961, p.84), paraphrasing Heidegger, describes the phenomenon of home as "an overwhelming, inexchangeable something to which we were subordinate and from which our way of life was oriented and directed, even if we had left our home many years before". Home is the foundation of our identity as individuals and as members of a community, the dwelling-place of being. Home is not just the house you happen to live in, it is not something that can be anywhere, that can be exchanged, but an irreplaceable centre of significance. This may seem very philosophical and obscure, but in fact it can be a common, everyday element of experience. This is illustrated in the following account made to Robert Coles (1972, p.358) by an old Appalachian farmer:

> "It's just not that much of a *home* here, a place that you have and your kin always have had and your children and theirs will have, until the end of time when God calls us all to account. This here place— it's a good house mind you—but it's just a place I got. A neighbour of my daddy's had it and he left it, and my daddy heard and I came and fixed it up, and we have it for nothing. We worked hard and put a lot into it, and we treasure it, but it never was a *home*, not the kind I knew and my wife did. We came back to the hollow but it wasn't like it used to be when we were kids and you felt you were living in the same place all your ancestors did. We were part of this land ..."

Home in its most profound form is an attachment to a particular setting, a particular environment, in comparison with which all other associations with places have only a limited significance. It is the point of departure from which we orient ourselves and take possession of the world. Oscar Handlin (1951, p.8) in his study of immigrants to the United States, writes:

> "... 'I was born in such a village in such a parish'—so the peasant invariably began the account of himself. Thereby he indicated the importance of the village in his being; this was the fixed point by which he knew his position in the world and his relationship with all humanity."

It is difficult if not impossible to maintain that this sort of attachment to a home place is characteristic of contemporary society. The Appalachian farmer cited above looked back to a house that was gone; Heidegger writes of home in the past tense and declares: "Home nowadays is a distorted and perverted phenomenon. It is identical to a house; it can be anywhere. It is subordinate to us; easily measurable and expressible in numbers of money-value" (Vycinas, 1961, pp.84–85). Possibly it is true that modern man is, as numerous existential philosophers and sociologists claim, a homeless being, and that there has been widespread loss of attachment to home places. But this dismissal of the significance of home by Heidegger is too sweeping; there are surely more stages of association with home places than complete attachment and complete unattachment. Furthermore the associations and commitments that do exist between people and their homes may be largely covered up by attitudes of materialism, and become apparent only in times of loss and hardship. Marc Fried (1963, p.151) a psychiatrist investigating the reactions of a group of residents from Boston's West End whose homes were expropriated and who were relocated elsewhere in the city, found that many of them had emotional responses that could "properly be described as grief ... including a sense of painful loss ... continued longing ... a sense of helplessness ... and a tendency to idealise the lost place". Harvey Cox (1968, pp.423–424) cites the example of a woman from Lidice, the Czech village destroyed by the Nazis, who admitted that the greatest shock she experienced, in spite of the death of husband and separation from her children, was to come over the crest of a hill and to find nothing left of the village—not even ruins. A similar example is given by R.J.Lifton (1967, p.29) in his study of the survivors of Hiroshima: a history professor described his reaction to the destruction thus—

> "I climbed Hijoyama Hill and looked down. I saw that Hiroshima had disappeared ... I was shocked by the sight ... . What I felt then and still feel now I just can't explain with words. Of course I saw many dreadful scenes after that—but that experience, looking down and finding nothing left of Hiroshima—was so shocking that I simply can't express what I felt."

Although in our everyday lives we may be largely unaware of the deep psychological and existential ties we have to the places where we live, the relationships are no less important for that. It may be that it is just the physical appearance, the landscape of a place that is important to us, or it may be an awareness of the persistence of place through time, or the fact that *here* is where we know and are known, or where the most significant experiences of our lives have occurred. But if we are really rooted in a place and attached to it, if this place is authentically our *home*, then all of these facets are profoundly significant and inseparable. Such home places are indeed foundations of man's existence, providing not only the context for all human activity, but also security and identity for individuals and groups. Eric Dardel (1952, p.56) has written:

> "Before any choice, there is this place which we have not chosen, where the very foundation of our earthly existence and human condition establishes itself. We can change places, move, but this is still to look for a place, for this we need as a base to set down Being and to realise our possibilities—a *here* from which the world discloses itself, a *there* to which we can go."

A deep relationship with places is as necessary, and perhaps as unavoidable, as close relationships with people; without such relationships human existence, while possible, is bereft of much of its significance.

3.8 The drudgery of place

In 1678 the word 'nostalgia' was coined by a Swiss medical student, Johannes Hofer, to describe an illness that was characterised by such symptoms as insomnia, anorexia, palpitations, stupor, fever, and especially persistent thinking of home (McCann, 1941). Although we might now use the term 'homesickness' as a synonym for nostalgia, it is a weak synonym, for Hofer and subsequent physicians of the seventeenth and eighteenth centuries believed that this was a disease that could result in death if the patient could not be returned home. Nostalgia demonstrates that the importance of attachment to place was once well-recognised. But we also find Robert Burton (1932, p.344) writing in the sixteenth century in his *Anatomy of Melancholy*: "... death itself, another hell ... to be tied to one place." Admittedly such confinement in a place was only one among the almost limitless causes of melancholia that Burton identified, but his remark does suggest that attachment to a place is not entirely a pleasurable experience. The places to which we are most committed may be the very centres of our lives, but they may also be oppressive and imprisoning.

There is a sheer drudgery of place, a sense of being tied inexorably to *this* place, of being bound by the established scenes and symbols and routines. As the ground of our everyday lives places must partake of what Henri Lefebvre (1971, p.35) has called "the misery of everyday life", with its tedious tasks, humiliations, preoccupations with basic necessities, its hardships, meanness, and avarice. There is not merely a fusion between person and place, but also a tension between them. Ronald Blythe (1969, pp.16–17) writes of a village in East Anglia:

> "Only a generation or so ago, a villager who had to 'go away to work' was obliged to give up the close-knit and meaningful village background of which he was an important part ... . Or conversely, village life became so suffocating and inhibiting because he had no way of occasionally getting away from it, that a young man would join the army or simply the age-old drift away from his home village which was also his prison."

Drudgery is always a part of profound commitment to a place, and any commitment must also involve an acceptance of the restrictions that place imposes and the miseries it may offer. Our experience of place, and especially of home, is a dialectical one—balancing a need to stay with a desire to escape. When one of these needs is too readily satisfied we suffer either from nostalgia and a sense of being uprooted, or from the melancholia that accompanies a feeling of oppression and imprisonment in a place.

3.9 Essence of place

A place is a centre of action and intention, it is "a focus where we experience the meaningful events of our existence" (Norberg-Schulz, 1971, p.19). Indeed events and actions are significant only in the context of certain places, and are coloured and influenced by the character of those places even as they contribute to that character. Cézanne, to use a favourite example of Merleau-Ponty, did not paint landscapes, he painted the landscapes of Provence.

Places are thus incorporated into the intentional structures of all human consciousness and experience. Intentionality recognises that all consciousness is consciousness of something—I cannot do or think except in terms of something (Husserl, 1958, pp.119–121). Human intention should not be understood simply in terms of deliberately chosen direction or purpose, but as a relationship of being between man and the world that gives meaning. Thus the objects and features of the world are experienced *in their meaning* and they cannot be separated from those meanings, for these are conferred by the very consciousness that we have of the objects. This is so regardless of whether we are selfconsciously directing our attention towards somethings or whether our attitude is unselfconscious.

Places are the contexts or backgrounds for intentionally defined objects or groups of objects or events, or they can be objects of intention in their own right. In the former context it might be said that all consciousness is not merely consciousness of something, but of something in its place, and that those places are defined largely in terms of the objects and their meanings. As objects in their own right, places are essentially focuses of intention, usually having a fixed location and possessing features which persist in an identifiable form. Such places may be defined in terms of the functions they serve or in terms of communal and personal experience. They can be at almost any scale, depending on the manner in which our intentions are directed and focused—as a nationalist my place is the nation, but in other situations my place is the province or region in which I live, or the city or the street or the house that is my home.

In short, those aspects of the lived-world that we distinguish as places are differentiated because they involve a concentration of our intentions, our attitudes, purposes and experience. Because of this focusing they are set apart from the surrounding space while remaining a part of it. Places are thus basic elements in the ordering of our experiences of the world; Max Scheler (cited in Matoré, 1962, p.16) wrote: "To find one's place in the world, the world must be a cosmos. In a chaos there is no place."

The basic meaning of place, its essence, does not therefore come from locations, nor from the trivial functions that places serve, nor from the community that occupies it, nor from superficial and mundane experiences —though these are all common and perhaps necessary aspects of places. The essence of place lies in the largely unselfconscious intentionality that defines places as profound centres of human existence. There is for virtually everyone a deep association with and consciousness of the places where we were born and grew up, where we live now, or where we have had particularly moving experiences. This association seems to constitute a vital source of both individual and cultural identity and security, a point of departure from which we orient ourselves in the world. A French philosopher, Gabriel Marcel, (cited in Matoré, 1966, p.6) has summarised this simply: "An individual is not distinct from his place; he is that place."

On the identity of places

There are two major reasons for attempting to understand the phenomenon of place. First, it is interesting in its own right as a fundamental expression of man's involvement in the world; and second, improved knowledge of the nature of place can contribute to the maintenance and manipulation of existing places and the creation of new places. The real difficulty lies, however, not in the justification of the study of place, but in the development of adequate concepts and approaches for this. These must be based on the recognition that, as Wagner (1972, p.49) expresses it: "Place, person, time and act form an indivisible unity. To be oneself one has to be somewhere definite, do certain things at appropriate times." Given this fusion of meaning, act, and context, it has sometimes been suggested that generalisations about places cannot be formulated. "Both region and writer, person and place, are unique", declares Hugh Prince (1961, p.22), "and it is in their distinctive qualities that we find their essential character." From this it follows that to capture, comprehend and communicate 'essential character' depends largely on artistic insight and literary ability. Such an approach is well illustrated in the work of many novelists and other artists, for example Ronald Blythe's *Akenfield* (1969), a study of an English village through the verbatim accounts of its inhabitants, or Lawrence Durrell's essays (1969) about the Greek Islands collected under the title *The Spirit of Place.* An alternative method is that of systematic and objective description and analysis in which places are considered only in terms of their general properties, for instance as gap towns, commuting centres, central places or points in isotropic space. In fact neither approach offers much towards an understanding of places as phenomena of experience: the former is too specific and the latter is too general. What is required is an approach and attendant set of concepts that respond to the unity of 'place, person, and act' and stress the links rather than the division between specific and general features of places.

It is the purpose in this chapter to examine one such set of concepts and methods relating to the notion of 'identity' of place. This examination is based on the recognition that while places and landscapes may be unique in terms of their content they are nevertheless products of common cultural and symbolic elements and processes (Wagner, 1972, p.5). Identity of place is as much a function of intersubjective intentions and experiences as of the appearances of buildings and scenery, and it refers not only to the distinctiveness of individual places but also to the sameness between different places.

4.1 The identity of places

The notion of identity is a fundamental one in everyday life. Heidegger (1969, p.26) has written: "Everywhere, wherever and however we are related to beings of every kind, identity makes its claim upon us." Thus we recognise the identities of people, plants, places, and even nations. Possibly because it is so fundamental, identity is a phenomenon that evades simple definition, although some of its main characteristics are apparent. In particular the difference yet relationship between 'identity of' and 'identity with' should be noted. The identity of something refers to a persistent sameness and unity which allows that thing to be differentiated from others. Such inherent identity is inseparable from identity with other things; Erik Erikson (1959, p.102), in a discussion of ego identity, writes: "The term identity ... connotes both a persistent sameness within oneself ... and a persistent sharing of some kind of characteristic with others." Thus identity is founded both in the individual person or object and in the culture to which they belong. It is not static and unchangeable, but varies as circumstances and attitudes change; and it is not uniform and undifferentiated, but has several components and forms.

Kevin Lynch (1960, p.6) defines the identity of a place simply as that which provides its individuality or distinction from other places and serves as the basis for its recognition as a separable entity. This tells us only that each place has a unique address, that it is identifiable. Ian Nairn (1965, p.78) offers some expansion of this: he recognises that "there are as many identities of place as there are people", for identity is in the experience, eye, mind, and intention of the beholder as much as in the physical appearance of the city or landscape. But while every individual may assign selfconsciously or unselfconsciously an identity to particular places, these identities are nevertheless combined intersubjectively to form a common identity. Perhaps this occurs because we experience more or less the same objects and activities and because we have been taught to look for certain qualities of place emphasised by our cultural groups. Certainly it is the manner in which these qualities and objects are manifest in our experience of places that governs our impressions of the uniqueness, strength, and genuiness of the identity of those places.

It is clear that rather than being a simple address in a gazetteer or a point on a map, identity is a basic feature of our experience of places which both influences and is influenced by those experiences. What is involved is not merely the recognition of differences and of samenesses between places—but also the much more fundamental act of identifying sameness in difference. And it is not just the identity *of* a place that is important, but also the identity that a person or group has *with* that place, in particular whether they are experiencing it as an insider or as an outsider.

In the following discussion identity is considered in terms of, first, the constituent components of the identity of places; second, forms and levels of outsideness and insideness, or identity with places; third, the links between individual, group, and mass images of places and the identities of those places; and finally, the ways in which identities develop, are maintained, and change.

4.2 The components of the identity of places

If we consider places only in terms of their specific content, they present a remarkable diversity—one in which common elements are not readily apparent. Furthermore, our experiences of places are direct, complete, and often unselfconscious; if there are component parts, they are experienced in the fullness of their combinations. However, from a rather less immediate perspective one can distinguish elements, bound together but identifiable nevertheless, that form the basic material out of which the identity of places is fashioned and in terms of which our experiences of places are structured. These are like the fundamental components of a painting—the canvas, the paint, the symbols, each irreducible to the other but inseparable. Albert Camus' essays on North Africa are used here to demonstrate the components of the identity of place, but almost any description or direct observation of a particular place would serve just as well.

In his essays on the life and landscape of Algeria Albert Camus (1955, 1959) uses a clearly structured approach in his accounts of places. Both when he is describing his own experiences and when he is describing as an observer he reveals not only what appear to be the basic components of the identity of all places, but also the interweaving of these. Consider for example his account of Oran (1955, pp.130–131):

> "Oran has its deserts of sand: its beaches. Those encountered near the gates are deserted only in winter and spring. Then they are plateaus covered with asphodels, peopled with bare little cottages among the flowers ... . Each year on these shores there is a new harvest of girls in flower. Apparently they have but one season ... . At eleven a.m., coming down from the plateau, all that young flesh, lightly clothed in motley materials, breaks on the sand like a multi-coloured wave ... . These are lands of innocence. But innocence needs sand and stones. And man has forgotten how to live among them. At least it seems so, for he has taken refuge in this extraordinary city where boredom sleeps. Nevertheless, that very confrontation constitutes the value of Oran. The capital of boredom besieged by innocence and beauty ..."

Here Camus makes quite clear the major features of the landscape around Oran. First there is the bountiful physical setting of sand, sea, and climate and buildings. This provides the backdrop to the ostensible, observable activities of the people, yet is complemented by and influences those activities. But embracing and infusing both of these is a set of meanings for Camus—particularly the opposition of innocence and boredom.

These three components of place that are so apparent in Camus' writings—the static physical setting, the activities, and the meanings— constitute the three basic elements of the identity of places. A moment's reflection suggests that this division, although obvious, is a fundamental one. For example it is possible to visualise a town as consisting only of buildings and physical objects, as it is represented in air photographs. A strictly objective observer of the activities of people within this physical context would observe their movements much as an entomologist observes ants, some moving in regular patterns, some carrying objects, some producing objects, some consuming objects, and so on. But a person experiencing these buildings and activities sees them as far more than this —they are beautiful or ugly, useful or hindrances, home, factory, enjoyable, alienating; in short they are meaningful. The first two of these elements can probably be easily appreciated, but the component of significance and meaning is much more difficult to grasp.

The meanings of places may be rooted in the physical setting and objects and activities, but they are not a property of them—rather they are a property of human intentions and experiences. Meanings can change and be transferred from one set of objects to another, and they possess their own qualities of complexity, obscurity, clarity, or whatever. All this is well illustrated in an example quoted by Stephan Strasser (1967, pp.508– 509). In 1084 St. Bruno went to the French Alps to establish himself as a hermit there. Before his arrival the environment was quite neutral to him; it was what it was without meaning. But by seeking in those mountains a place to meditate St. Bruno and his followers made them meaningful in terms of this intention—they became 'dangerous' or 'safe', 'useful', or 'inhospitable'. And subsequently as their intentions changed, as they found a suitable site and began to look for land for cultivation, or as his followers now try to get rid of troublesome tourists, so their situation was modified. In other words the meaning of the situation, of the place, was defined by the intentions of St. Bruno and his followers. This is, of course, a very straightforward example; meaning is much more complex than this for intentionality is itself very complicated, involving both individual and cultural variations which reflect particular interests, experiences and viewpoints. But the example of St. Bruno does serve to demonstrate that places can only be known in their meanings.

The three fundamental components of place are irreducible one to the other, yet are inseparably interwoven in our experiences of places. In explicating this experience, however, they can be identified as distinctive poles or focuses, and they can be further subdivided within themselves. Thus the physical component can be understood as comprising earth and sea and sky, and a built or created environment, each of which offers its own characteristic possibilities for experience (Dardel, 1952). Similarly activities and functions can be distinguished as being creative or destructive or passive, as communal or individual. The relative weighting of each of these subcomponents may be of considerable importance in establishing the identity of particular places—thus we recognise coal-mining towns or mountain villages. Artists, photographers, and novelists may even compress identity into one small feature which somehow captures the essence of a place; Wallace Stegner (1962) found that for him the spirit of his former home town of Whitemud on the Prairies was expressed above all in the smell of wolf-willow.

Such selection or concentration of the identity of a place into one feature depends, of course, on local circumstances and on the purposes and experiences of the author, and is not especially relevant to the present, more general discussion. What is significant here is the way in which physical setting, activities, and meanings are always interrelated. Like the physical, vital, and mental components of behaviour that Merleau-Ponty (1967) identifies, it is probable that they constitute a series of dialectics that form one common structure. Physical context and activities combine to give the human equivalent of locations within the 'functional circle' of animals (see Cassirer, 1970, p.26); setting and meanings combine in the direct and empathetic experience of landscapes or townscapes; activities and meaning combine in many social acts and shared histories that have little reference to physical setting. All of these dialectics are interrelated in a place, and it is their fusion that constitutes the identity of that place. Physical appearance, activities, and meanings are the raw materials of the identity of places, and the dialectical links between them are the elementary structural relations of that identity.

This analysis of the components of identity of place is not, however, complete. There is another important aspect or dimension of identity that is less tangible than these components and dialectics, yet serves to link and embrace them. This is the attribute of identity that has been variously termed 'spirit of place', 'sense of place' or 'genius of place' (*genius loci*)—all terms which refer to character or personality. Obviously the spirit of a place involves topography and appearance, economic functions and social activities, and particular significance deriving from past events and present situations—but it differs from the simple summation of these. Spirit of place can persist in spite of profound changes in the basic components of identity. Rene Dubos (1972, p.7) writes: "Distinctiveness persists despite change. Italy and Switzerland, Paris and London have retained their respective identities through many social, cultural and technological revolutions." The spirit of place that is retained through changes is subtle and nebulous, and not easily analysed in formal and conceptual terms. Yet at the same time it is naively obvious in our experience of places for it constitutes the very individuality and uniqueness of places. D. H. Lawrence (1964, p.6) wrote:

> "Different places on the face of the earth have different vital effluence,
> different vibration, different chemical exhalation, different polarity
> with different stars; call it what you like. But the spirit of place is a
> great reality."

4.3 Insideness and outsideness

The major components of the identity of place do not apply solely to
places, but are to be found in some forms in all geographies, landscapes,
cities, and homes. The essence of place lies not so much in these as in the
experience of an 'inside' that is distinct from an 'outside'; more than
anything else this is what sets places apart in space and defines a particular
system of physical features, activities, and meanings. To be inside a place
is to belong to it and to identify with it, and the more profoundly inside
you are the stronger is this identity with the place.

Norberg-Schulz (1971, p.25) has written that "to be inside is the
primary intention behind the place concept; that is to be somewhere,
away from what is outside". In a similar vein Lyndon (1962, pp.34–35)
has suggested that basic to place is the creation of an inside that is
separate from an outside: "Being inside is knowing where you are." It is
the difference between safety and danger, cosmos and chaos, enclosure
and exposure, or simply here and there. From the outside you look upon
a place as a traveller might look upon a town from a distance; from the
inside you experience a place, are surrounded by it and part of it. The
inside–outside division thus presents itself as a simple but basic dualism,
one that is fundamental in our experiences of lived-space and one that
provides the essence of place.

The manifestations of the difference between inside and outside are
many and obvious—the walls of buildings and of old cities, town limit
signs, national frontiers, phrases such as 'in town' and 'out of town'. In
this context the significance of doors, gateways, and thresholds becomes
quite clear. Eliade (1959, p.18 and p.25) summarises it: "The threshold
concentrates not only the boundary between inside and outside but also
the possibility of passage from one to the other." But it is at precisely
this point that Bachelard's warning (1969, p.211 and pp.217–218) takes
on significance: "Outside and inside form a dialectic of division, the
obvious geometry of which blinds us ... . Outside and inside are both
intimate—they are always ready to be reversed, to exchange their
hostility." Thus, to take a mundane example, we go out to the city into
the countryside, yet return again into the city. In fact the dualism of
inside and outside is not quite as clear as it appears at first sight.

In part this reversal of inside and outside occurs because each of us
becomes "the centre of a sort of mental space, arranged in concentric
zones of decreasing interest and decreasing adherence" (Gabriel Marcel,

cited in Tuan, 1971, p.185). These zones are defined by our intentions; if our interest is focused on our home then everything beyond home is outside, if our concern is with our local district then everything beyond that district is outside, and so on. In short, as our intentions vary, so the boundary between inside and outside moves. In consequence there are many possible levels of insideness. Furthermore, to some degree we carry these zones around with us as we move, we are always at the centre of our perceptual space and hence in a place. This egocentric structuring of space helps to blur any sharp division between inside and outside that may be presented by physically or culturally defined boundaries. And these physical boundaries may themselves be blurred—medieval city walls were surrounded by *faubourgs*, modern cities fade through suburbia, subtopia, and exurbia into the countryside, and architects and planners offer us, in Cullen's phrase (1971, p.28), "indoor landscapes and outdoor rooms".

The lack of clarity in the distinction between inside and outside can be understood, in part at least, as a function of the different levels of intensity with which we experience outsideness and insideness. A number of such levels can be identified, and while these are not discrete and precisely separated they can be recognised as more or less distinctive ways of experiencing places. Peter Berger (1971, pp.20–21) distinguishes three levels of the assimilation of anthropologists into the cultures which they study: (i) behavioural—engaging in the activities of the culture while remaining a dispassionate observer; (ii) empathetic—involving emotional as well as behavioural participation, while retaining an awareness of not being a full member of the culture; (iii) cognitive or 'going native', in which case it ceases to be possible to do cultural anthropology. Although this classification has a specifically methodological context it does suggest the possibility of similar breakdowns of insideness in places. Thus there is behavioural insideness—or physical presence in a place; empathetic insideness which involves emotional participation in and involvement with a place; and existential insideness[5], or complete and unself-conscious commitment to a place. These are all modes of experience that are immediate and direct, but there are also other modes that are less immediate: vicarious insideness refers to the experience of places through novels and other media; through incidental outsideness places are merely backgrounds for other activities; from the perspective of objective outsideness places are treated as concepts and locations; and existential outsideness involves a profound alienation from all places.

[5] The term 'existential insideness' is used here to avoid confusion with the term 'cognitive space' used elsewhere in this book. Clearly 'cognitive' as employed by Berger has the same sense as 'existential' in this context.

4.3.1 Existential outsideness

> "The new city was still to me as though denied and the unresponsive
> landscape spread its darkness as though I were not there. The nearest
> things did not bother to reveal themselves to me. The alley climbed to
> the street light. I saw how alien it was" (Rilke, cited in Pappenheim,
> 1959, p.33).

Rilke's poem expresses a rejection of an individual by a place which he
is condemned always to observe as though from outside. There is an
awareness of meaning withheld and of the inability to participate in those
meanings. This is the condition of existential outsideness that has
fascinated so many nineteenth and twentieth century novelists and poets.

Existential outsideness involves a selfconscious and reflective uninvolve-
ment, an alienation from people and places, homelessness, a sense of the
unreality of the world, and of not belonging. From such a perspective
places cannot be significant centres of existence, but are at best
backgrounds to activities that are without sense, mere chimeras, and at
worst are voids. Thus Proust's comment (1970, p.288) that "the places
we have known belong now only to the little world of space on which we
map them for our convenience". And Henry Miller's harsh assessment
(1947, p.xv) of America:

> "America is full of places. Empty places. And all these empty places
> are crowded. Just jammed with empty souls. All at loose ends, all
> seeking diversion. As though the chief objects of existence were to
> forget. Everyone seeking a nice cosy little joint to be with his fellow
> man and not with the problems which haunt him. Not ever finding such
> a place, but pretending that it does exist. If not here then elsewhere."

In existential outsideness all places assume the same meaningless identity
and are distinguishable only by their superficial qualities.

4.3.2 Objective outsideness

The deliberate adoption of a dispassionate attitude towards places in order
to consider them selectively in terms of their locations or as spaces where
objects and activities are located, involves a deep separation of person and
place. Selfconsciously places are changed from facts of immediate
experience into things having certain attributes, within systems of locations
that can be explained by 'central place theory' or some other theory of
location. This attitude of objective outsideness has a long tradition in
academic geography and is particularly apparent in implicit beliefs that
geography is some type of integrating superscience or that there is a real
objective geography of places that can be described once and for all.
"Geographies", says the geographer in St. Exupery's *The Little Prince*
(1943, p.65), "are the books which, of all books, are most concerned with
matters of consequence. They never become old-fashioned   We write

of eternal things." For many geographers such comment is close to the
truth, though the objective cataloguing of information satirized by St.
Exupery has now been largely replaced by what Bartels (1973, p.25) calls
'instrumental rationality'. This requires the "neutralisation of thought
against subjective peripheral influences" in order to explain in a scientific
manner the spatial organisation of places.

A similar intellectual posture is adopted by many planners in making
studies for proposals for reorganising places. This enables them to separate
themselves emotionally from the places which they are planning and to
restructure them according to principles of logic, reason, and efficiency.
"This may be compared", writes Cullen (1971, p.194), "to God creating
the world as someone outside and above the thing created".

4.3.3 Incidental outsideness

While objective outsideness is in essence a deliberately adopted intellectual
attitude, incidental outsideness describes a largely unselfconscious attitude
in which places are experienced as little more than the background or
setting for activities and are quite incidental to those activities. This type
of experience is described by Melvin Webber (1964, p.113) in his
discussion of "the non-place urban realm": "In his role as a member of a
world-wide community of virus researchers, the scientist is not a member
of a place community at all. The fact that his laboratory is located in a
given town or metropolis may be almost irrelevant to maintaining the
crucial links with men in other places." A similar account could be made
of businessmen going from city to city merely to attend conferences and
meetings, or of flight crews and truck drivers for whom the places visited
are of little importance in themselves. Indeed such incidental outsideness
is probably a feature of everyone's experience of places, for it is inevitable
that what we are doing frequently overshadows where we are doing it, and
pushes places into the background. And even the most intense encounters
with place are fleeting unless some deliberate effort is made to maintain
that encounter (Tuan, 1974, pp.93–94).

Incidental outsideness applies only to those places in which we are
visitors and towards which our intentions are limited and partial. In our
home places it is, conversely, the case that whatever we do and however
our intentions may focus on social events and activities, we are 'incidental
insiders'.

4.3.4 Vicarious insideness

It is possible to experience places in a secondhand or vicarious way, that
is, without actually visiting them, yet for this experience to be one of a
deeply felt involvement. One purpose of the artist or poet in depicting a
place is to convey something of what it is to live there, to give a sense of
that place. David McCord (Museum of Fine Arts, 1970, p.11) writes in his
introduction to a catalogue of Andrew Wyeth's paintings: "Poets, painters,

and musicians sometimes choose to live, and strictly operate, within a very special world defined by very special boundaries self-imposed. They do not set out to discover these worlds: they appear to be born within them ... . When we read, inspect or listen to their work we enter into their domain ..." Through travel accounts or motion pictures or any other medium, we can indeed enter far into other worlds and other places that are sometimes real and sometimes fantasy. Wyeth's paintings take us into the small areas of Pennsylvania and Maine where he lives, while Wright's *Islandia* (1942) can convey us to a wholly imaginary world and make it appear real. The degree to which we are transported and the identity of those places to which we are transported depends presumably both on the artist's skills of description and on our own imaginative and empathetic inclinations. But possibly vicarious insideness is most pronounced when the depiction of a specific place corresponds with our experiences of familiar places—we know what it is like to be *there* because we know what it is like to be *here*.

4.3.5 Behavioural insideness

Behavioural insideness consists of being in a place and seeing it as a set of objects, views, and activities arranged in certain ways and having certain observable qualities. In contrast to incidental outsideness in which a place is experienced as little more than a background to events, behavioural insideness involves deliberately attending to the appearance of that place. Such insideness is clearest when it is complemented by surrounding walls, by enclaves or enclosures, or other physically defined boundaries. It is probably in this relatively narrow sense that insideness is most commonly understood.

In itself behavioural insideness tells us merely that we are somewhere, but it is the patterns, structures and content of this inside that tell us we are *here* rather than somewhere else. These patterns are, in the first instance, those of our immediate experience, and perhaps the most important element of this is sight. Certainly it is the best understood aspect of place experience, with the other senses reinforcing or being interpreted by reference to visual patterns. It is primarily these visual patterns that are considered here in describing behavioural insideness and its role in the identity of places.

In his investigation of townscape Gordon Cullen (1971, pp.193–194) examines the places of our immediate experience, and seeks "to chart the structure of the subjective world" and to explore "the art of the environment". He attempts this by investigating our reactions to the relationships between buildings, spaces, objects, and activities, and by classifying and illustrating various modes of these relationships. There are, Cullen believes, essentially three elements in our experiences of environment: first is 'place', by which he means something broadly equivalent to the French term '*place*', our immediate position defined visually as an enclave or enclosure; second is 'content', appearance in all its facets, including the nature of this and that, colour, texture, scale, style, and character; and third is 'serial vision', the sequence of views as we move into, out of, and between 'places', a constant interplay of the anticipated and the revealed view that binds together the various static 'places' and their content. The patterns formed by these elements are infinitely varied though structured into relations of here and there, and this and that. The essential point in all this is the simple one that "the items of the environment cannot be dissociated one from the other" (Cullen, 1971, p.189), though of perhaps more importance here is the fact that it is the manner of the association of these items and the physical qualities of appearance that give particular places unique identities in our experiences of them as behavioural insiders.

4.3.6 Empathetic insideness

There is no abrupt distinction between empathetic and behavioural insideness, rather there is a fading from the concern with the qualities of appearance to emotional and empathetic involvement in a place. This is not inevitable for, as Tuan (1971, p.190) observes, "bodily presence may be necessary, but it is not sufficient to guarantee experience". In short, empathetic insideness demands some deliberate effort of perception.

Steen Rasmussen (1964, p.40) has described the difference between seeing a picture of a place and then visiting it, but his description could apply just as well to the difference between just being in a place and being in a place and opening one's senses to all that place has to offer:

> "Anyone who has seen a place in a picture and then visited it knows how different the reality is. You sense the atmosphere all around you and are no longer dependent on the angle from which the picture was made. You breathe the air of the place, hear its sounds, notice how they are reechoed by the unseen houses behind you."

Empathetic insideness demands a willingness to be open to significances of a place, to feel it, to know and respect its symbols—much as a person might experience a holy place as sacred without necessarily believing in that particular religion. This involves not merely looking at a place, but *seeing* into and appreciating the essential elements of its identity[6]. Such empathetic insideness is possible for anyone not constricted by rigid patterns of thought and who possesses some awareness of environment.

To be inside a place empathetically is to understand that place as rich in meaning, and hence to identify with it, for these meanings are not only

---

[6] The distinction between 'looking' and 'seeing' (i.e. between behavioural and empathetic insideness) is made by Adolf Portmann (1959) and by Paul Shepard (1967). This distinction should not be interpreted as one between science and art; 'seeing' is just as important for the scientist as for the artist, and 'looking' is simply the superficial form of observing that characterises standardised and institutional science or glib and commercialised art.

linked to the experiences and symbols of those whose place it is, but also stem from one's own experiences. Thus the identity of places experienced through empathetic insideness is much deeper and richer than that known only through behavioural insideness. Identity is not just an address or set of appearances, but a complete personality with which the insider is intimately associated. Such identity of place does not present itself automatically, but must be sought by training ourselves to see and understand places in themselves; to paraphrase a statement about architecture made by Rasmussen (1964, p.236): "... if we ourselves are open to impression and sympathetically inclined the place will open up and reveal its true essence."

4.3.7 Existential insideness
To be inside a place and to experience it as completely as we can does not mean that existentially we are insiders. The most fundamental form of insideness is that in which a place is experienced without deliberate and selfconscious reflection yet is full with significances. It is the insideness that most people experience when they are at home and in their own town or region, when they know the place and its people and are known and accepted there. Existential insideness characterises belonging to a place and the deep and complete identity with a place that is the very foundation of the place concept.

Existential insideness is part of knowing implicitly that *this* place is where you belong—in all other places we are existential outsiders no matter how open we are to their symbols and significances. Thus Bruce Hutchison (1943, p.36) writes of Quebec City: "It is the houses, not the monuments, squares, and public buildings that hold the life of Quebec ... . But it must forever escape the stranger, so that looking at the shuttered window, the bolted door, he can only sense it, like a distant perfume, like the sound of voices behind a garden gate, forever closed to him." The person who has no place with which he identifies is in effect homeless, without roots. But someone who does experience a place from the attitude of existential insideness is part of that place and it is part of him. Then there exists between place and person a strong and profound bond like the tie between farmer and property expressed by the dirt farmer in John Steinbeck's *The Grapes of Wrath* (1969, p.39):

> "Funny thing how it is. If a man owns a little property, that property is him, it's part of him, and it's like him. If he owns property only so he can walk on it and handle and be sad when it isn't doing well and feel fine when the rain falls on it, that property is him, and in some way he's bigger because he owns it. Even if he isn't successful he's big with his property. That is so."

4.4 Images and identities of places

Although it is possible to gain considerable insights into the nature of
identity of places by considering its main components, it is nonetheless
clear that identity is not a product of such components alone, but is
socially structured. In other words, identity varies with the individual,
group, or consensus image of that place. Indeed, for most purposes it
appears that the image of a place *is* its identity and that to understand
something of the social structure of images is an essential prerequisite for
understanding identity.

An image has been defined by Boulding (1961) as a mental picture that
is the product of experiences, attitudes, memories, and immediate sensations.
It is used to interpret information and to guide behaviour, for it offers a
relatively stable ordering of relationships between meaningful objects and
concepts. Images are not just selective abstractions of an objective reality
but are intentional interpretations of what is or what is believed to be.
The image of a place consists of all the elements associated with the
experiences of individuals or groups and their intentions toward that place.
Insofar as these intentions are focused and are specific, such images may
be considered by others to be narrow and biased, but for those who hold
them they are complete and constitute the reality of that place.

Images of places have both a vertical and a horizontal structuring. The
vertical structure is one of intensity and depth of experience and has
layers corresponding basically to those of the various levels of outsideness
and insideness. The horizontal structure is that of the social distribution
of knowledge of places within and between individuals, groups, and the
mass.

4.4.1 Individual images of place

Within one person the mixing of experience, emotion, memory, imagination,
present situation, and intention can be so variable that he can see a
particular place in several quite distinct ways. A street is a very different
place to a pedestrian and to a car driver—they do not even attend to the
same objects and signs and they certainly have quite different experiences
and purposes—yet at different times one person may both walk and drive
down that street (see Luijpen, 1966, pp.67–68; Kockelmans, 1966,
pp.81–84). In fact for one person a place can have many different
identities. How, or whether, such differences are reconciled is not clear,
but it is possible that the relatively enduring and socially agreed upon
features of a place are used as some form of reference point.

Between individuals even sharper distinctions of attitudes to place exist.
James Boswell (cited in Briggs, 1968, p.83) once declared that "I have
often amused myself with thinking how different the same place is to
different people", and indeed every individual does have a more or less
distinctive image of a particular place. This is not only because each
individual experiences a place from his own unique set of moments of

space–time, but more especially because everyone has his own mix of
personality, memories, emotions, and intentions which colours his image
of that place and gives it a distinctive identity for him. Ernst Cassirer
(1970, pp.160–161) gives the example of the painter Ludwig Richter who
set out with three of his friends to paint the identical landscape in
Tuscany while staying as close to its reality as possible: "Nevertheless
the result was four totally different pictures, as different from one another
as the personalities of the artists." In the same way the identity of a
place varies with the intentions, personalities, and circumstances of those
who are experiencing it.

4.4.2 Group or community images of place

It has been suggested (Lowenthal, 1961, p.248) that "a consummate piece
of combinatorial mathematics" enables these diverse personal images to be
brought together into a common social image of place. But this is
misleading for it assumes that all individual images are independent.
This is not the case—individual images have been and are being constantly
socialised through the use of common languages, symbols, and experiences
(Berger and Luckmann, 1967, pp.130–132 and pp.32–36). Furthermore
the identities of places are founded, like all images, on the interaction of
what Gurvitch (1971, p.xiv) calls the three opposing poles of the *I*, the
Other, and the *We*: "The I's communicate with the Other principally
through the medium of signs and symbols of which the only possible basis
is the We, which gives them effective validity. To wish to separate the I,
the Other and the We, is to desire to dissolve or to destroy consciousness
itself ..." The common basis of the We is not, however, constant, but
varies in intensity and depth. The most intense degree of union is attained
when images are completely combined through a profound intersubjective
linking; this is sociality in communion, and it gives to places an identity
like that given by existential insideness or the sacred experience of holy
places—deeply personal yet shared. Where there is a lesser penetration of
images but "an essential part of the aspirations and acts of personality is
integrated into the We", sociality is community; and when the fusion of
images is weak and superficial it is sociality in mass giving mass identities
to places.

The level of community lies between the scales of the individual and
the mass at the stage of what Berger and Luckmann (1967, pp.163–173)
term "secondary socialisation"—that of group attitudes, interests, and
experiences. Communities and groups are not, however, the same;
communities may adopt the structure of groups, but are spontaneous and
fluctuating social forms of knowledge, whereas groups are formal and
organised. Yet through interest groups such communities can develop and
an image be projected in which the identities of places of significance to
that group are a reflection of group interests and biases. Thus a particular
city presents a different identity to those living in its slums, its ghettos,

its suburbs; and to developers, planners, and citizens' action groups. Such differences in identity are never more apparent than in confrontations between different groups. Thus, in an archetypal development-preservation conflict, the valley of Hetch-Hetchy was, for the water engineers of San Francisco, an excellent potential source of water that could only be enhanced by damming and flooding; but for the Sierra Club this was a wild place of spiritual significance, a sanctuary and a temple, that could only be destroyed by development (Nash, 1967).

In short, for different groups and communities of interest and knowledge, places have different identities. Personal eccentricities and attitudes are subsumed to the dominant image of the groups, perhaps to gain either the functional and political benefits or the sense of personal security of group membership.

4.4.3 Consensus and mass images of place

Although one particular place may have quite different identities for different groups, there is nevertheless some common ground of agreement about the identity of that place. This is the consensus identity of a place, in effect its lowest common denominator. It appears to take two forms, and, following the terms of C. W. Mills (1956, pp.298–324), these are the public and the mass identities.

The public identity is that which is common to the various communities of knowledge in a particular society, and comprises the more or less agreed on physical features and other verifiable components of places. It is a consensus because it has developed out of the free opinion and experience of groups and individuals, although descriptive regional geography in providing facts about places may constitute much of the basis of such a consensus identity. But in essence the public identity of place is merely a particularly pervasive form of sociality in community at a rather superficial level of integration of interest, and one which ties together group images of places.

In contrast are mass identities of places. Rather than developing out of group and individual experiences, mass identities are assigned by 'opinion-makers', provided ready-made for the people, disseminated through the mass-media and especially by advertising. They are the most superficial identities of place, offering no scope for empathetic insideness and eroding existential insideness by destroying the bases for identity with places. This is so because mass identities are based not on symbols and significances, and agreed on values, but on glib and contrived stereotypes created arbitrarily and even synthetically.

Mass media conveniently provide simplified and selective identities for places beyond the realm of immediate experience of the audience, and hence tend to fabricate a pseudo-world of pseudo-places. And someone exposed to these synthetic identities and stereotypes will almost inevitably be inclined to experience actual places in terms of them—a fact not missed by the developers of such real-life pseudo-places as Waikiki or Disneyland.

Jeremy Sandford and Roger Law (1967, p.89) observe that "package-trip British tourists see nothing strange in the fact that hundreds and hundreds of miles of the Mediterranean seaboard have been built up in the image of their dreams ...", and the same could be said of innumerable tourist centres, shopping districts and even residential areas. In effect both the image and the actual physical setting have been manipulated and manufactured so that they correspond, and the result is a superficial and trivial identity for places which increasingly pervades all our experiences of places and which can only be transcended by a considerable intellectual or social effort.

4.5 The development and maintenance of identities of places

It is easy to visualise a person who visits a town for the first time developing an image of that town which comprises a number of centres of varying significance linked by particular routes. But this is misleading, for it implies that he begins with something akin to a *tabula rasa* and that the identity of that place for him develops solely out of observation and experience. In fact the process of identity construction appears to consist of a complex and progressive ordering and balancing of observations with expectations, *a priori* ideas with direct experiences, until a stable image is developed.

This process of structuring our knowledge of the world has been especially well described by Jean Piaget (1968, 1971). He suggests (1968, pp.7–8) that all human action consists of a balancing of the processes of assimilation and accommodation.

> "... All needs tend first of all to incorporate things and people into the subject's own activity, i.e. to 'assimilate' the external world into the mental structures that have already been constructed; and secondly to readjust these structures as a function of subtle transformations, i.e. to 'accommodate' them to external objects."

He argues that knowledge does not begin with a knowledge of the self or of things as such, but with a knowledge of their interactions. It is by progressing simultaneously towards both poles of assimilation and accommodation, by reconciling new knowledge with the old and old knowledge with the new, that intelligence organises the world.

In the context of place the most obvious implication of this is that identities of places cannot be understood simply in terms of patterns of physical and observable features, nor just as products of attitudes, but as an indissociable combination of these. The identity of a place is an expression of the adaptation of assimilation, accommodation, and the socialisation of knowledge to each other. And for most purposes it is 'ultrastable', that is to say that, no matter how these three factors may vary, the identity will continue to provide at least a minimally adequate guide for physical survival and social acceptability (Ashby, 1965, chapter 7). In other words there are no places that have no identity.

For the existential insider this process of balancing assimilation and accommodation is, of course, quite unselfconscious, for there is a gradual and subtle development of an identity with and of his place that begins in childhood and continues throughout life. For the person who is "prepared to expose himself to the new experience of a place and ask himself what that place is doing to him and how it is doing it" (Gauldie, 1969, p.184), that is for the empathetic insider, the balance of assimilation and accommodation is the selfconscious purpose. The extent to which it can be achieved depends both on his ability to step outside his own cultural and personal values, and on his sensitivity of observation. But for outsiders, those who experience a place only in terms of a crass level of behavioural insideness and who know only its mass identity, preconceptions and established attitudes always outweigh direct experience. Observations are fitted into the ready-made identities that have been provided by mass media or into *a priori* mental schemata, and inconsistencies with these are either ignored or explained away.

Once it has been developed, whether by an individual, a group, or the mass, an identity of a place will be maintained so long as it allows acceptable social interaction and has plausibility—that is, so long as it can be legitimated within the society (Berger and Luckmann, 1967, pp.92–108). Where an identity has developed through experience in communion or in community it will endure for as long as the symbols and significances of that place retain their meanings. In primitive societies, those without history, this is effectively for ever; and even in vernacular societies identities of places change but slowly, over generations rather than years. But the mass identity is legitimated less by appeal to effective symbols than to 'objective' reality in the form of photographs and factual descriptions. Insofar as this objective reality can be manipulated to suit the interests of the identity-makers, the mass identity itself can be changed.

There are two main ways in which an identity of a place can cease to be plausible. First, changing environmental conditions can render it inadequate for the purposes of social interaction and individual behaviour, just as a scientist who clings to a disproved theory may eventually find it impossible to continue his research as conflicting evidence builds up. And second, changes in attitude, fashion, or other aspects of belief systems, can render an image implausible; thus an industrial town with factories and smoke stacks might have once been seen as a centre of progress and production, but following the awakening of an 'environmental consciousness' is now more likely to be considered a centre of pollution and ecological destruction. There appear to be no fixed points of implausibility, nor is the change from one identity to another usually abrupt—rather there is a gradual and variable change.

The identities linked to the superficial qualities of place, that is mass identities, are rendered implausible more easily than those associated with existential and empathetic insideness. This is simply because the manipulation of mass knowledge and attitude through the mass media is more possible than shifts in the symbolic and significant properties of places. Mass identity is indeed little more than a superficial cloak of arbitrarily fabricated and merely acceptable sets of signs. It provides no roots, no sense of belonging to a place. It is in marked contrast to those place-identities which have developed through profound individual and social experiences and which constitute enduring and recognisable 'territories of symbols' (Klapp, 1969, p.28).

4.6 Types of identities of places

The identity of a place is comprised of three interrelated components, each irreducible to the other—physical features or appearance, observable activities and functions, and meanings or symbols. There is an infinite range of content within each of these and numberless ways in which they can combine. Hence there is no discernible limit to the diversity of identities of places, and every identifiable place has unique content and patterns of relationship that are expressed and endure in the spirit of that place.

But it is not feasible to argue that uniqueness and the individuality of identity are the only important facts in our experiences of places. While each place is unique and has a persistent sameness within itself, at the same time it shares various characteristics with other places. In terms of our experiences this sharing does display certain consistences that make it possible to distinguish a number of types of identities of places.

1. From the individual perspective or sociality in communion of existential insideness places are lived and dynamic, full with meanings for us that are known and experienced without reflection.

2. For empathetic insiders, knowing places through sociality in community, places are records and expressions of the cultural values and experiences of those who create and live in them.

3. From the standpoint of behavioural insideness place is ambient environment, possessing qualities of landscape or townscape that constitute a primary basis for public or consensus knowledge of that place.

4. In terms of incidental outsideness it is usually selected functions of a place that are important and the identity of that place is little more than that of a background for those functions.

5. The attitude of the objective outsider effectively reduces places either to the single dimension of location or to a space of located objects and activities.

6. The mass identity of place is a consensus identity that is remote from direct experience for it is provided more or less ready-made by the mass media. It is a superficial identity, for it can be changed and manipulated like some trivial disguise so long as it maintains some minimum level of credibility. It is also pervasive, for it enters into and undermines individual experiences and the symbolic properties of the identities of places.

7. For existential outsiders the identity of places represents a lost and now unattainable involvement. Places are all and always incidental, for existence itself is incidental.

With the exception of existential outsideness which replaces all the others, these various types of identity are not discrete, nor mutually exclusive, nor unchanging. Thus we may know our home town as dynamic and full of meaning, yet be quite capable of also viewing it as professional planners or geographers from the perspective of objective outsideness, and also participate in its mass identity. For each setting and for each person there are a multiplicity of place identities reflecting different experiences and attitudes; these are moulded out of the common elements of appearance and activities and the borrowed images of the media through the changing interactions of direct observation with preconceptions.

The identity of place is not a simple tag that can be summarised and presented in a brief factual description. Nor can it be argued that there is a real or true identity of a place that relates to existential insideness. Indeed an outsider can in some senses see more of a place than an insider—just as an observer of argument gains a perspective not available to those arguing, even though he misses the intensity of being involved in that argument. Identity is, in short, neither an easily reducible, nor a separable quality of places—it is neither constant and absolute, nor is it constantly changing and variable. The identity of place takes many forms, but it is always the very basis of our experience of *this* place as opposed to any other.

A sense of place and authentic place-making

Ian Nairn (1965, p.6) has written:

> "It seems a commonplace that almost everyone is born with the need
> for identification with his surroundings and a relationship to them—
> with the need to be in a recognisable place. So sense of place is not a
> fine art extra, it is something we cannot afford to do without."

The most meagre meaning of 'sense of place' is the ability to recognise
different places and different identities of a place. But while this is
important for orientation and even survival, Nairn is clearly referring to
something more complex and profound than the capacity to differentiate
localities. He is suggesting the importance of a sense of identity with a
place and what Harvey Cox (1968, p.423) has described as "the sense of
continuity of place necessary to people's sense of reality". In fact there
exists a full range of possible awareness, from simple recognition for
orientation, through the capacity to respond empathetically to the
identities of different places, to a profound association with places as
cornerstones of human existence and individual identity.

It is the intention in this and the following chapter to examine some of
the forms of sense of place and 'placelessness', and to describe some of the
manifestations of these in landscapes. Sense of place may be authentic
and genuine, or it can be inauthentic and contrived or artificial. These
notions of authenticity and inauthenticity are taken from phenomenology,
but they are ideas which have, under a variety of slightly different guises,
had long currency. In particular, former notions of 'sincerity' bear a close
resemblance to authenticity (Trilling, 1971); and John Ruskin's conception
(n.d., p.143) of the 'true life' and the 'false life' serves very well to
convey the meaning of authenticity and inauthenticity:

> "Man's true life ... is the independent force by which he moulds and
> governs external things; it is a force of assimilation which converts
> everything around him into food, or into instruments; and which ...
> never forfeits its own authority as a judging principle. His false life is,
> indeed, but one of the conditions of death or stupor, but it acts, even
> when it cannot be said to animate, and it is not always easily known
> from the true; it is that life of custom and accident in which many of
> us pass much of our time in the world ... that life which is overlaid by
> the weight of things external to it, and is moulded by them instead of
> assimilating them ...".

This authentic–inauthentic division provides the basis for the following
discussion, but it does not necessarily offer a complete framework for the
description of all experiences of places, nor is intended that these
categories are absolute. Rather it is the foundation for an interpretation,

and, just as Nietzsche (1955) observed that truth can come from error or good from evil, it is recognised that authenticity may come from inauthenticity or vice versa, and that these two modes of experience are not always clearly differentiable. These reversals and complexities are not stressed, however, and the simple division between sense of place and placelessness is emphasised for the sake of clarity.

5.1 Authentic sense of place

In his book *Sincerity and Authenticity* Lionel Trilling (1971) argues that in Shakespeare's time sincerity was the avoidance of being false to any man by being true to one's own self, but that the term 'sincerity' has subsequently been debased and in part replaced by 'authenticity', though this latter term suggests a more strenuous moral experience. However, authenticity still connotes that which is genuine, unadulterated, without hypocrisy, and honest to itself, not just in terms of superficial characteristics, but at depth. In the more precise but more obscure terms of existentialism 'authenticity' refers to a mode of being, *Dasein*, which recognises a man's freedom and responsibility for his own existence (Heidegger, 1962, p.68 and p.220 ff.). It is held that a man's possibilities are his own, for he is directly present to the world, and in authentic existence a person lives his or her life in full awareness of this basic and inescapable relationship. Nevertheless these possibilities are in part communal, for the actions we take are necessarily taken within a social context (Tymieniecka, 1962, p.182). An authentic person is thus one who is sincere in all he does while being involved unselfconsciously in an immediate and communal relationship with the meanings of the world, or while selfconsciously facing up to the realities of his existence and making genuine decisions about how he can or cannot change his situation. Such a person stands in fundamental contrast to someone who either denies the fundamental realities of his existence, or explains them away as acts of Fate, the Will of God, the dictates of history, environment, economics, fashion, or whatever. Whereas the authentic person assumes responsibility for his existence, the inauthentic person transfers responsibility to large, nebulous, unchangeable forces, for which he cannot be blamed and about which he can do nothing.

An authentic attitude to place is thus understood to be a direct and genuine experience of the entire complex of the identity of places—not mediated and distorted through a series of quite arbitrary social and intellectual fashions about how that experience should be, nor following stereotyped conventions. It comes from a full awareness of places for what they are as products of man's intentions and the meaningful settings for human activities, or from a profound and unselfconscious identity with place.

5.1.1 Unselfconscious sense of place

In unselfconscious experience an authentic sense of place is rather like the type of relationship characterised by Martin Buber (1958) as 'I–Thou', in which the subject and object, person and place, divisions are wholly replaced by the relationship itself, for this is complete and mutual. It has often been suggested that this type of relationship to places is most strongly developed in "unspoiled primitive people, partly because their survival depends on knowing the right fishing place and the good pasture, and partly because their world is peopled with inexplicable forces which make one place lucky and another place unlucky and which have to be propitiated" (Gauldie, 1969, p.171). The world is peopled with place-spirits and ties to places are spiritual rather than physical. But while it is possible to accumulate numerous examples of a deep sense of a place in such cultures, it is misleading to imply that there is a clear division between primitive and other levels of technological sophistication in terms of an unselfconscious experience of environment. "The modern urbanite", writes Paul Shepard (1967, p.42), "is astonished at the ability of the native hunter to move long distances in his territory without getting lost, though he may go about his city unconsciously observing clues in the same way."

Yet it can be maintained that there is a difference between primitive and modern cultures—a difference in the complexity and intensity of meanings attached to places. Most of us no longer live in a world inhabited by spirits and their symbols, nor even in a world in which there are significant holy places. For the Australian aborigine space is sacred and places are unique focuses of sacredness, but for contemporary man even when space is unselfconsciously experienced it is primarily functional and secular and places are merely interchangeable locations. That there has been a relative desacralising and desymbolising of the environment seems undeniable, particularly for everyday life. But for many people there may still exist deep psychological links with place, links that only become apparent under conditions of stress. Harvey Cox (1968, p.422) suggests that there are many people "who never fully recover" from the loss of "continuity of relationships with places" that results from urban renewal projects; and the not infrequent dramatic attempts by residents and homeowners to resist developers, even though they may have been offered better physical accommodation elsewhere, are indicative of these deep relationships with place (see Pawley, 1971, pp.98–107).

An authentic sense of place is above all that of being inside and belonging to *your* place both as an individual and as a member of a community, and to know this without reflecting upon it. This might be so for home, for hometown or region, or for the nation. Such an authentic and unselfconscious sense of place is perhaps as important and necessary in contemporary societies as it was in any previous societies, for it provides an important source of identity for individuals, and through them for communities. But however great the need for such a sense of place may be, the possibility of its development for many people in technologically advanced cultures has been undermined by the possibility of increased spatial mobility and by a weakening of the symbolic qualities of places. And while for the primitive hunter or medieval artisan a sense of belonging to his place imbued his whole existence, for the modern city-dweller it is rarely in the foreground and can usually be traded for a nicer home in a better neighbourhood.

5.1.2 Selfconscious sense of place

In unselfconscious experience places are innocently accepted for what they are; in selfconscious experience they become objects of understanding and reflection—the relationship is, in Buber's terms as modified by Harvey Cox (1965, pp.48–49), changed from 'I-Thou' to 'I-You'. Although the latter relationship is perhaps more superficial and the union between subject and object is not complete, a considerable intensity of association with places is still possible. The 'I-You' relationship is essentially that of the outsider or stranger who seeks to experience places as openly as possible, to respond to their unique identities. It is based perhaps on the recognition that, to adapt Sinclair Gauldie's statement (1969, p.1) about architecture, "somewhere above the level of brute survival, places can communicate delight, surprise, wonder or horror, and the ability to attend knowledgeably to such communications enhances life". To 'attend knowledgeably' here means an explicit "act of judgement, a comparison of the new experience with one's expectations", and an attempt to open one's senses to all the aspects of a particular place and to experience it both empathetically and sympathetically. Of course it does not follow that everyone who achieves the same measure of openness experiences the identical place, for identity is determined in part by the intentions and experiences of the observer. Instead, this suggests some form of geographical idealism, an attempt to experience all the qualities and meanings of a place both as the people living there might experience them and also in terms of their functional, aesthetic, or other qualities that might not be apparent to existential insiders. The more open and honest such experiences are, and the less constrained by theoretical or intellectual preconceptions, the greater is the degree of authenticity.

But places can also be experienced in a direct and very personal way by outsiders that does not involve such efforts of 'idealism'. This is *genius loci*: "a living ecological relationship between an observer and an environment, a person and a place", a source of self-knowledge and a point of reference that is possibly most important in childhood, but which can provide a centre of personal stability and significance throughout life (Cobb, 1970, p.125). It is perhaps the ability to convey this quality that characterises authors and artists with a 'sense of place'. Regionalism and regional writing are often little more than a "vehicle of sentimentality in which the incompetents choose to travel ..." (Grigson, 1972, p.859), and the place is effectively outside the writer. But a region is *inside* the writer with a sense of place, and what he writes is not superficial description, but has significance that goes beyond this locality and speaks to the actual or potential *genius loci* of everyone. For Albert Camus (1955, p.144) this type of profound relationship with a place was achieved with the ruins at Tipasa in Algeria. It was to these he returned after an absence of many years in order to discover that "... to keep from shrivelling up like a beautiful orange containing nothing more than a bitter dry pulp ... one must keep intact in oneself a freshness, a cool wellspring of joy, love the day that escapes injustice and return to combat having won that light".

5.2 Authentically created places

While places acquire meaning simply because we live in them, their architecture and man-made landscape are not superfluous, for human life requires a system of places that have structure and form and meaning (Norberg-Schulz, 1969, p.226). Such a system of distinctive places can be created both on the basis of an unselfconscious and a selfconscious sense of place. The former is expressed through an unselfconscious design procedure which is based primarily on the use of traditional solutions to traditional problems; it tends to give rise to places that reflect the total physical, social, aesthetic, spiritual, and other needs of a culture, and in which all those elements are well adapted to each other (Alexander, 1964). The selfconscious and authentic sense of place is associated with a design process that is goal oriented and may involve finding innovative solutions to problems; it is founded on a complete conception of man and his relationship to the gods and nature, and on the possibilities of expressing this in particular settings[7]. The result is usually places which possess both internal harmony and which fit their context.

It is possible to identify categories of authentically made places in an abstract way, but it is not necessarily possible to find examples of particular places which illustrate those categories perfectly. The photographs accompanying the following text are not therefore illustrations of purely authentic place-making, but do demonstrate cases in which authenticity seems to have been a major element even though artifice and inauthenticity may be apparent in some degree. In this respect the photographs do not simply illustrate the text, but hopefully amplify and qualify it by indicating some of the inevitable complexities in the manifestations of the attitudes of place-making.

---

[7] This is the type of ontology examined by Martin Heidegger (Vycinas, 1961). It was discussed in part in chapter 3, especially sections 3.7 and 3.8.

5.2.1 Places made unselfconsciously

It was suggested above that an authentic and unselfconscious sense of place is as important in contemporary as in primitive societies. However accurate such a statement may be in terms of the *need* for a sense of place, it certainly does not follow that the places created in technologically advanced cultures are made as authentically as those of primitive or even vernacular cultures. Gauldie (1969, p.171; see also Cox, 1965, chapter 8) suggests that for primitive peoples "practical and superstitious feelings about place go hand in hand, for the working life, the religious life, and the place are not split apart". There exists, in fact, a total and unified experience of place, and this experience is manifest through a design process which consists of the "... direct and unselfconscious translation into physical form of a culture, its needs and values—as well as the desires, dreams and passions of the people" (Rapoport, 1969, p.2 and p.5). It is characterised by a lack of theoretical or aesthetic pretension, a working with site and climate, a respect for other people and their buildings, and hence for the complete environment both man-made and natural, and it functions in terms of well-proven forms that admit only limited variations (figure 5.1). The end result is places which fit their context and are in accord with the intentions of those who created them, yet have a distinct and profound identity that results from the total involvement of a unique group of place-makers with a particular setting. Evidence for this is admirably provided in Bernard Rudofsky's photographic essay, *Architecture without Architects*; his illustrations of villages and landscapes demonstrate the harmony and 'humanness' that can result from an authentic and unselfconscious sense of place.

In so-called post-industrial societies an unselfconscious design process remains important, at least in terms of the quantity of objects that result from it. Doxiadis (cited in Jencks, 1971, p.49) has estimated that only about twenty per cent of the buildings in the world are even influenced by architects, and while individual buildings or objects are designed, their combinations in places are rarely preconceived. However, in cultures in which mass-values and mass communications are prevalent there can be few buildings or places which are not influenced by mass fashion or professional designs. Indeed in North America the only instances of authentically yet unselfconsciously created places are peripheral to the main thrust of the society, for instance the anachronistic and traditional societies of the Hutterites or Amish, and possibly some 'back-to-nature' communes and some street markets. In Europe authentically created landscapes and places are essentially relict features of former craft cultures. In both continents such landscapes have acquired nostalgic value (Newcomb, 1972) and are zealously being preserved or even recreated, hence guaranteeing their inauthenticity.

Figure 5.1. Authentically and unselfconsciously made places: Castle Combe, Wiltshire and Vieille Brioude, Auvergne.

"The direct and unselfconscious translation into physical form of a culture, its needs and values" (Rapoport, 1969, p.2).

Figure 5.2. Places which have gained authenticity by being lived-in: Treorchy, South Wales and Kensington Market, Toronto.

"Street after regular street of shoddily uniform houses ... but to the insider these are small worlds, each as homogeneous and well-defined as a village" (Hoggart, 1959, p.52).

But we should not be too anxious to classify most of the modern western world as comprising inauthentic places, for unselfconscious place-making cannot be considered a single, instantaneous occurrence. Even though the founding of a place may be its most dramatic and significant event, place-making is a continuous process and the very fact of having been lived-in and used and experienced will lend many places a degree of authenticity. Nicholas Taylor (1973, p.193), writing of the undistinguished interwar suburbs of English cities, observes that "the homecentred nuclear family can have a feeling within itself that it belongs somewhere, in a definite place: unique people within a unique environment, with powers of real responsibility for ordering their own lives". And of course this is right. What appears from the outside to be homogeneous and placeless, is from within closely differentiated into places by the personalisation of property, by association with local events and the development of local myths and by being lived in, all of which give a genuineness and authenticity to somewhere quite inauthentically created, be it a subdivision of mass-produced Tudorbethan houses or a high-rise apartment building (figure 5.2). Yet such 'authentification' can never be complete for it can never reach the deepest levels of sense of place. The difference is like that between making your own painting and acquiring a reproduction which you then frame—there may be some sense of personal achievement and involvement but it can never be total. It is to this sense of incompleteness that Kevin Lynch (1972, p.41) is referring when he writes: "Most Americans still live in second-hand homes, but the homes are not their own. And so they go away to Europe to feel at home in time."

5.2.2 Places made selfconsciously

An authentic and selfconscious sense of place is manifest in attempts to create places that reflect a clear and complete conception of man as well as a sensitivity to the significance of place in everyday life. It is often the prerogative of elite groups and individuals rather than an articulated expression of the values of all members of a community. It is difficult to find examples of authentically created places that are completely consistent, but the following do illustrate some of the more important features of such places.

(i) "For a brief generation in Athens", writes Lewis Mumford (1961, p.166), "the ways of the gods, the ways of nature and the ways of men came close to a common point." In the Hellenic period Athens was itself an expression of generally held beliefs in the beauty yet usefulness of nature, in an earth designed by the gods and in which Greece possessed the ideal environment, and in the freedom of the citizens. "For a while city and citizens were one, and no part of life seemed to be outside their formative, self-molding activities"; this was truly an authentic city in which intentions, activities, and physical form were completely bound together, and while in part the form of Athens may have evolved

Figure 5.3. An authentically and selfconsciously made place: Ancient Athens.

"For a brief generation in Athens the ways of the gods, the ways of nature and the ways of men came close to a common point" (Mumford, 1961, p.166).

unselfconsciously, the conceptions of man, nature, and the gods that stood behind it, and the siting and design of many of the buildings, were quite selfconscious (figure 5.3). The clearest expression of this was in the building of the temples. Scully (1962, p.213) writes:

> "The Greek architect ... dealt with forms both natural and constructed. With them he celebrated his three deathless themes: the sanctity of the earth, the tragic stature of mortal life upon the earth, and the whole natures of those recognitions of the facts of existence which are the gods."

(ii) A rather different case of authentic place-making is demonstrated in the building of the cathedral at Chartres, and perhaps a little less dramatically in the other Gothic cathedrals and churches of Europe. In contrast to the evolution of Hellenic Athens, the form and siting of these were entirely deliberate and preconceived by a master builder. But they did derive from a conception of man and man's relation to God that was universally accepted. Built in the twelfth century, the cathedral at Chartres was not just the work of master craftsmen, but "... the faithful harnessed themselves to the carts which were bringing stones and dragged them from the quarry to the cathedral ... . Amongst them were lords and ladies, pulling carts with the rest. There was perfect discipline and a most profound silence. All hearts were united." (Clark, 1969, p.56). The cathedral was indeed built by common effort and through a total involvement, both physical and spiritual, with the project. The 'cult of the carts' can be dismissed as merely another example of an upsurgence of Christian zeal (Henderson, 1968, pp.34–37), but the results at Chartres and elsewhere were cathedrals and abbeys which were an expression of a total faith, a manifestation of an I–Thou relationship between man and God, and between man and the earth as the home of God. Perhaps it was for this reason that almost without exception Gothic religious architecture satisfied the requirements of beauty stipulated by St. Thomas Aquinas— 'a certain wholeness or perfection', 'a due proportion or harmony', and 'clarity' (cited in Allsopp, 1970, p.35). And these requirements were satisfied not just in the buildings themselves but also in the way in which they combined with settings in the landscape or townscape (figure 5.4). Chartres demonstrates well the intensity of the commitment that lay behind Gothic religious place-making, but all the buildings that arose from this intention reflect a selfconscious ability to create authentic places.
(iii) The authenticity of place-making in the early part of the Renaissance was founded on principles of humanism rather than religious involvement. Geoffrey Scott (1961, p.120) argues that Renaissance architects possessed a "humanist passion which made architecture the counterpart of all moods of the spirit". They recognised that we transcribe ourselves in terms of architecture and transcribe architecture in terms of ourselves, and armed with a humanistic conception of man that was taken from the Greeks and

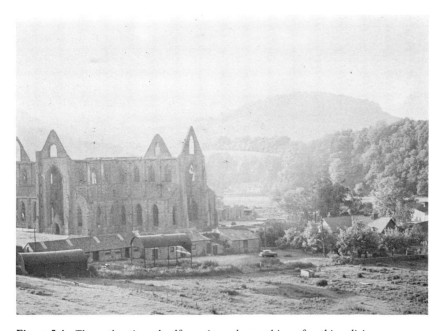

Figure 5.4. The authentic and selfconscious place-making of gothic religious architecture: Chartres Cathedral (left) and Tintern Abbey.

Manifestations of an I–Thou relationship between man and God, and between man and the earth as the home of God.

a considerable engineering ability they produced an architecture and town-planning that was quite authentic in its attempts to express man's humanity (figure 5.5). Nevertheless this authentic place-making was limited—it was that of a small elite of artists supported by the wealth of merchants and the Church, and it scarcely reflected the interests and values of all the people. After perhaps only two generations of artists and architects this authentic architecture began to become both aesthetically and intellectually pretentious. The grand piazzas and wide avenues, the monumental buildings, may have been products of a tradition that was originally humanistic, but they became increasingly flamboyant and overt expressions of prestige, wealth, and power (Mumford, 1961, p.166).
(iv) Authentic place-making, even by elite groups, has become increasingly unlikely since the Renaissance. Nevertheless attempts to found Utopian communities, such as those of Robert Owen or Etienne Cabet, possessed some measure of authenticity. They were all based on a more or less complete conception of man and society, and were attempts to create communities in which all the parts functioned harmoniously. But of course most of these communities were short-lived—they were either split by internal dissension or succumbed to external pressures. Furthermore,

"they were models of generosity and sympathy, quite different from the ideal cities of the Renaissance", which were models of humanity and order (Benevolo, 1967, p.84 and p.129). The motives and values behind them were not so much humanistic as humanitarian, philanthropic and political. Owen's 'New Harmony', or the Rappite colony of 'Economy' were indeed technical experiments, and while their conception may have been based on a broad image of what society should be like, their realisation was very much a reflection of limited, largely inauthentic, industrial models and techniques[8].

(v) Pioneers and settlers coming to North America from Europe in the nineteenth century were in many cases not merely escaping from oppressive social and economic conditions, but were making a decisive break with the place they had been born and raised (see Handlin, 1951). Those who carved their own new home out of the bush were in effect reestablishing their roots—they were making a place authentically through their own labour and through a commitment to a new way of life. The log cabin in the clearing was an expression of hope, of total involvement and of responsibility for the decision to emigrate (figure 5.6). J. Sheridan Hogan, in an essay which won first prize from the Paris Exhibition of Canada in 1855 (Cross, 1970, p.72), wrote:

Figure 5.5. Authentically and selfconsciously made places of the Renaissance: Florence. Expressions of "the humanist passion which made architecture the counterpart of all moods of the spirit" (Scott, 1961, p.120).

[8] Fourier's 'Phalanstery' or Godin's 'Familistère' in particular give the impression that they were efficient factories for the production of living, and Bentham even called his model prison an 'Industry-House Establishment' (Benevolo, 1967).

"That little clearing ... which to others might afford such slender guarantee for bare subsistence, was nevertheless a source of bright and cheering dreams to that lonely settler. He looked at it, and instead of thinking of its littleness, it was the foundation of great hopes of a large farm and rich corn fields to him."

Of course this is a rather romantic picture and there was blatant commercialism, corruption and materialism on the frontier, and in creating their authentic places the settlers were very often destroying the authentic places of Indians. But for the settlers themselves the founding of a home in the wilderness was a genuine and authentic act, regardless of how involved they later became with production and economy or how picturesque and fashionable they made the farm.

(vi) In contemporary society such authentic and selfconscious place-making seems to be reserved largely for inspired individuals; most of us are condemned to live in other peoples' houses and machine-made places. But architects such as Alvaar Aalto and Frank Lloyd Wright have sometimes demonstrated an acute sense of place; of Wright's desert homes, especially Taliesin West, Gauldie (1969, pp.172–173) has written that he did not

Figure 5.6. An authentic place made through personal commitment: A settler's hut on the Opeongo Road, Ontario, 1901 (courtesy of Macnamara Collection, Public Archives of Ontario).

"The clearing, which to me was a mere ugly picture on the retina, was to them a symbol redolent with moral memories and sang a very paean of duty, struggle and success" (William James, 1899, pp.151–152).

merely imitate native dwellings:

> "... rather he seems to have passed the significant elements of the
> landscape through the crucible of his own deep feeling for place and
> his own powerful imagination and to have produced from them some
> virtue which gives the building its own sense of belonging."

With the exception of the work of such talented individuals modern
selfconscious design has tended to result in places which are single-purpose,
functionally efficient, often in a style independent of the physical setting,
reflecting mass values and contrived fashions. The present trend appears
to be away from a variety of authentically created places which reflect an
interaction of diverse intentions and values with a respect for physical
settings and landscapes, towards non-place urban realms, international
landscapes and placelessness.

5.3 Authenticity and place

As a form of existence authenticity consists of a complete awareness and
acceptance of responsibility for your own existence. But in terms of the
experience and creation of places authenticity rarely appears in such a
pure form—instead it is discontinuous and occurs with different levels of
intensity. An 'I-Thou' experience of place is a total and unselfconscious
involvement in which person and place are indissociable; such relationships
are probably uncommon and certainly difficult to achieve in contemporary
societies. However, an 'I-You' relationship with place, in which there is a
genuine response to the meanings, symbols and qualities of a place and an
attempt to identify with it, is more possible. Indeed it is this relationship
that must be encouraged if we are to begin to see and appreciate places
for what they are, and not in terms of mass values, or technical and
intellectual attitudes and conventions.

As places can be experienced with different intensities of authenticity,
so they can be created with varying degrees of authenticity. At the extreme
there is the total expression of a culture through an unselfconscious design
tradition, and the selfconscious attempt to express man's condition and
humanity that is so well illustrated in Greek architecture. But authentic
place-making seems to have become decreasingly probable on a community
scale since Hellenic times, and now seems to be vested largely within
individuals. The probability may have declined but the possibility and the
need for such genuine selfexpression in places still exists. August Heckscher
(cited in Brett, 1970, p.140) has written:

> "What the individual requires ... is not a plot of ground but a *place*—a
> context within which he can expand and become himself. A place in
> this sense cannot be bought; it must be shaped, usually over long
> periods of time, by the common affairs of men and women. It must
> be given scale and meaning by their love. And then it must be preserved."

6

Placelessness

There is a widespread and familiar sentiment that the localism and variety
of the places and landscapes that characterised preindustrial societies and
unselfconscious, handicraft cultures are being diminished and perhaps
eradicated. In their stead we are creating, in Norberg-Schulz's (1969)
terse phrase, 'a flatscape', lacking intentional depth and providing
possibilities only for commonplace and mediocre experiences. C. W. Moore
(in Lyndon, 1962, pp.33–34) has written that "the richly varied places of
the world ... are rapidly being obliterated under a meaningless pattern of
buildings, monotonous and chaotic"; and Gordon Cullen (1971, p.59)
suggests of Britain that "we appear to be forsaking nodal points for a
thinly spread coast-to-coast continuity of people, food, power and
entertainment; a universal wasteland ... a chromium-plated chaos". Such
comments indicate the possibility of a placeless geography, lacking both
diverse landscapes and significant places, and also imply that we are at
present subjecting ourselves to the forces of placelessness and are losing
our sense of place.

Cultural and geographical uniformity is not, of course, an entirely new
phenomenon. The spread of Greek civilisation, the Roman Empire,
Christianity, or even the diffusion of the idea of the city, all involved the
imposition of a homogeneity on formerly varied cultures and landscapes.
What is new appears to be the grand scale and virtual absence of
adaptation to local conditions of the present placelessness, and everywhere
the shallowness of experience which it engenders and with which it is
associated. Alexis de Tocqueville (1945, II, p.240) identified in the 1830s
the character of this uniformity:

> "Variety is disappearing from the human race; the same ways of acting,
> thinking, and feeling are to be met with all over the world. This is not
> only because nations work more upon each other and copy each other
> more faithfully, but as the men of each country relinquish more and
> more the peculiar opinions and feelings of a caste, a profession, or a
> family, they simultaneously arrive at something nearer to the
> constitution of man, which is everywhere the same. Thus they become
> more alike, even without having imitated each other."

Such a focusing on 'the constitution of man' does not, for Tocqueville,
involve high aspirations, but a levelling-down to a "countless multitude of
beings, shaped in each other's likeness, amid whom nothing rises and
nothing falls" (p.350). The present significance of these remarks lies in
their implication that while placelessness does comprise look-alike
landscapes that result from improved communications and increased
mobility and imitation, behind these lies a deep-seated attitude that
attends to the common and average characteristics of man and of place.

This 'inauthentic attitude of placelessness' is now widespread—to a very considerable degree we neither experience nor create places with more than a superficial and casual involvement.

It is easy to condemn this attitude and its manifestations as generally undesirable, to criticise it as an unfortunate but necessary concomitant of modern technology and society. But such criticisms are neither wise nor accurate. In all societies at all times there has been some placelessness, and insofar as lack of care for places provides a context and comparison it is essential for a sense of place.

Furthermore superficial expressions of placelessness are far from being an infallible guide to deeper attitudes; being lived-in confers some authenticity on even the most trivial and unrelentingly uniform landscapes. Richard Hoggart (1959, p.52) describes a nineteenth century industrial town in England: "To a visitor they are understandably depressing, these massed proletarian areas; street after street of shoddily uniform houses intersected by a dark pattern of ginnels and snickets (alleyways) and courts ... . But to the insider, these are small worlds, each as homogeneous as a village." In short, it is easy but erroneous to simplify placelessness, to see it everywhere in the post-industrial world, to advocate its removal by better planning and design. What is important is to recognise that placelessness is an attitude and an expression of that attitude which is becoming increasingly dominant, and that it is less and less possible to have a deeply felt sense of place or to create places authentically.

6.1 Inauthenticity

As authenticity consists of an openness to the world and an awareness of the human condition, so inauthenticity is an attitude which is closed to the world and to man's possibilities. Both are equally valid as modes of being and existence, and Heidegger (1962, p.68) takes pains to stress that inauthenticity is of *no lower order* than authenticity—it is simply a *different* order. Inauthenticity is not only as necessary and as viable in human existence as authenticity, but it is characteristic of normal and everyday life—we do as others do without reflection because it is the accepted way of behaviour. In practice, however, it is difficult to maintain this degree of objectivity and not to judge inauthenticity negatively, for inauthentic existence is stereotyped, artificial, dishonest, planned by others, rather than being direct and reflecting a genuine belief system encompassing all aspects of existence.

Inauthenticity is expressed especially through the "dictatorship of the 'They' (*das Mann*). We take pleasure and enjoy ourselves as '*they*' take pleasure; we read, see and judge literature and art as '*they*' see and judge." (Heidegger, 1962, p.168). This involves a levelling down of the possibilities of being, a covering-up of genuine responses and experiences by the adoption of fashionable mass attitudes and actions. The values are those of mediocrity and superficiality that have been borrowed or handed down from some external source. "In this world of inauthenticity", writes John Wild (1955, p.130 and p.132), "new and divergent insights are discounted as already long familiar. One knows it already. The exceptional is always levelled down to the average".

But this is only one form of inauthenticity—the largely unselfconscious and subjective form in which the individual is unwittingly governed by the 'anonymous they' without reflection or concern about this. There is also a second form that is more selfconscious and deliberate—the inauthenticity that is linked with the objective and artificial world of the 'public' (Olson, 1962, pp.135-136). Here objects are manipulated for the public interest and decisions are taken in a world of assumed, homogeneous space and time. "It makes all the difference in the world", Nietzsche (cited in Passmore, 1968, p.470) wrote, "whether a thinker stands in personal relation to his problems, in which he sees his destiny, his need and his higher happiness, or can only feel and grasp them impersonally, with the tentacles of cold, prying thought". Uncommited 'cold, prying thought' which characterises the philosophical approaches of positivism, and the technical approaches of much physical and social planning, is clearly inauthentic because of its very detachment and narrowness. Sartre (1948, pp.98-99) describes such inauthenticity in terms of a person masquerading as a waiter—he may do his job well and with considerable flair and ability, but the job is of no real importance to him, he does not feel personally engaged and committed to it. This form of inauthenticity is manifest particularly in what Jacques Ellul (1967) calls *technique*[9], that is an overriding concern with functional efficiency, objective organisation, and manipulative planning. Through *technique* attention is directed to objects and busyness and care for things, to the best way of achieving narrowly defined ends. Inevitably the technician manipulating the world of the public loses sight of the "overarching personal structures which give things meaning and ceases to look for meaning in his own existence" (Wild, 1959, p.104). He subsumes his individuality and that of others to a set of procedures which are determined by the technical nature of social engineering and planning.

It is clear that inauthenticity is the prevalent mode of existence in industrialised and mass societies, and it is commonplace to recognise that mass values and impersonal planning in all their social, economic, and

[9] This French term has no direct equivalent in English. It means rather more than 'technology' and incorporates the whole ethos that what you do is somehow less important than how you do it. If Ellul's analysis is accepted then *technique* is seen as perhaps the most pervasive and influential force in modern life, one which cannot be countered except by occasional individual rejection (cf the discussion on authentic place-making above). It should be noted that Ellul does not consider *technique* to be a particularly recent phenomenon in origin—it is to be found in all cultures which practise invention—but he does argue that it has undergone a great expansion since the eighteenth century and now penetrates all aspects of life (Ellul, 1967, chapter 6 and pp.64 ff.).

physical forms are major manifestations of such inauthenticity. But how these appear in the experience and appearance of places and landscapes is rarely considered. In the following section an attempt is made to outline the main features of an inauthentic attitude to places, the various ways in which such an attitude is transmitted, and its manifestations in place and landscape.

6.2 Inauthentic attitudes to place

An inauthentic attitude to place is essentially no sense of place, for it involves no awareness of the deep and symbolic significances of places and no appreciation of their identities. It is merely an attitude which is socially convenient and acceptable—an uncritically accepted stereotype, an intellectual or aesthetic fashion that can be adopted without real involvement. In inauthentic experience places are seen only in terms of more or less useful features, or through some abstract *a priori* model and rigid habits of thought and behaviour; above all such experiences are casual, superficial, and partial.

Inauthentic attitudes to place may be unselfconscious, stemming from an uncritical acceptance of mass values; or they may be selfconscious and based on a formal espousal of objectivist techniques aimed at achieving efficiency. The former are discussed here in the context of 'kitsch', particularly as it is displayed in attitudes towards 'home' and the attitudes of tourists; the latter are considered with reference to *technique* in planning.

6.2.1 Kitsch

Strictly the term 'kitsch' refers to the mediocre, styleless, sweetly sentimental, meretricious objects that are sold as souvenirs and gifts, and to their related forms in household goods, music, architecture, and literature. But there is a distinct kitsch style and kitsch attitude that stands behind these goods. Abraham Moles (1971, p.7) has identified the main features of this attitude; he suggests that kitsch is a way of being, a major part of everyday life in all affluent societies where many people can afford the trivial, the showy, and the ersatz, but present in all societies to some extent. It consists especially of a relationship between man and objects in which the objects are created and produced solely for consumption by a mass public. It is an attitude reflected in *gemütlichkeit*, quaintness, cuteness, artificiality, and it results in mediocrity and 'phoniness', rather than excellence and honesty.

Kitsch is apparent in places in many ways. As a set of forms and objects it is to be seen at all levels—from garden gnomes, to Ponderosa Steak Houses with artificial plastic cacti, to Minuteman Motels with model missiles, to the overindulgences of Baroque decoration, to roadside fantasylands and enchanted forests. As an attitude it is apparent in *Heimweh* and the sentimentalisation of home, and the needs and experiences of tourists in mass. In fact kitsch is an attitude of inauthenticity in which places are treated as things from which man is largely aliented, and in which the trivial is made significant and the significant is made trivial, the fantastic is made real, the authentic debased and value is measured almost entirely in terms of the superficial qualities of cost, colour, and shape.

Home. In authentic experience 'home', whether a house, a village, a region, or a nation, is a central point of existence and individual identity from which you look out on the rest of the world. To build a new house or to settle in a new territory is a fundamental project, equivalent perhaps to a repetition of the founding of the world. In primitive and vernacular cultures both practical and religious feelings about place are interwoven, and there is a deep and multi-faceted attachment to a single, clearly defined home area. But in contemporary society for many people "the working life, the home life, the religious life, and the place" are split apart (Gauldie, 1969, p.171); home is the location of your house and that can be changed every three or four years with little or no regret. Eliade (1959, pp.56–57) takes Le Corbusier's statement that a house is "a machine to live in" and writes: "You can change your machine to live in as often as you change your bicycle, your refrigerator, your automobile. You can also change cities or provinces without encountering any difficulties other than those which arise from a difference in climate" (figure 6.1). Such an interchangeability of 'homes'—it has been estimated that in North America the rate of mobility is equivalent to each household moving once every three years—is both made possible by and reinforces the reduction in the significance of 'home'.

The meaning of 'home' has been weakened not only through increased mobility and a splitting of the functions associated with it, but also by sentimentalisation and commercialisation. There is a wealth of kitschy bric-a-brac exploiting the general home-sweet-home theme, a theme captured especially well in the German notions of *Heimweh*, or homesickness, and *Heimat*. Leonard Doob (1964, p.66) gives the following translation from an Austrian almanac: "When we say this dear word '*Heimat*', then a warm wave passes over our hearts; in all our loneliness we are not alone and in all our sorrow we are not without comfort." And commercial interests have lost little time in exploiting the idea of home. A monolithic apartment company in Toronto advertises: "If you want a place to call home, call us", and real estate agents have virtually ceased to deal in houses. Instead they sell expensive homes, exclusive homes, apartment homes, townhomes. 'Home' has indeed become a marketable, exchangeable, and sentimentalised good.

Tourism. An inauthentic attitude to place is nowhere more clearly expressed than in tourism, for in tourism individual and authentic judgement about places is nearly always subsumed to expert or socially accepted opinion, or the act and means of tourism become more important than the places visited. Rasmussen (1964, p.16) writes of tourists visiting

Figure 6.1. Machines to live in: The trailer park at Elliot Lake, Ontario, and new housing in suburban Toronto.

"You can change your machine to live in as often as you change your bicycle, your refrigerator, your automobile" (Eliade, 1959, p.50).

the church of Santa Maria Maggiore in Rome: "... they hardly notice the character of the surroundings, they simply check off the starred numbers in their guide books and hasten on to the next one. They do not experience the place." This is inauthenticity at its most explicit; the guided tour to see those works of art and architecture that someone else has decided are worth seeing. It is found not only in the planeloads and busloads of tourists being conducted from sight to site across Europe, but also in such sophisticated guide books as the *Guides Verts Michelin*. These rank views, towns, villages, even frescoes, in a convenient three star classification so that everyone can know just how beautiful, exceptional or worth visiting a place is (figure 6.2). As Barthes (1972, pp.74–77) has pointed out, such guides stress the picturesque and the monumental; they rarely mention plains or plateaus and "the human life of a country disappears to the exclusive benefit of its monuments". Such inauthenticity is often intensified by personal narrowness of interest and by rigid adherence to cultural prejudices. The former is apparent in intellectuals and academics travelling to look only at Renaissance paintings or to measure cephalic indices or to study leaf forms; the latter is apparent in the attitudes of the package-trip British tourists in Spain quoted by Jeremy Sandford (1967, pp.43, 49):

> "The principal reason for Continental travel is, it's a status symbol. The people next door do it, so you do it too."
> "I'm taking quite a number of presents home for them as didn't come, as I think is only fair. I got a bullfight poster for my two nephews, with their names written in just like real bullfighters. I got a flamenco dancer with a bulb inside that lights up. I got fans with pictures of the Spanish mountains, and two old Toledo swords very reasonable."
> "Down a dark alley in Palma a notice says: 'Tea Pot 10 pts'. Next door: 'English Chips'. Then 'English Beer'."

It seems that for many people the purpose of travel is less to experience unique and different places than to collect those places (especially on film). It is this that is responsible for forcing the active tourist frontier into ever more remote and 'exotic' corners of the earth. This is social tourism, travel for social ends rather than experience, and its ultimate form is that expressed by Benjamin West (cited in Briggs, 1968, p.81)—the painter who felt he had no reason to go to Greece because he had read a catalogue of its main points of interest. In a similar way the motorised campers of North America and Europe, with their multiroomed tents and trailers equipped with television, showers and even built-in campfires, and travelling from one standardised campsite to another, are in effect making tourism itself unnecessary, for they are taking with them a part of their 'home' which happens to be mobile and which insulates them against the strangeness of new and different places (Lowenthal, 1970). In these cases

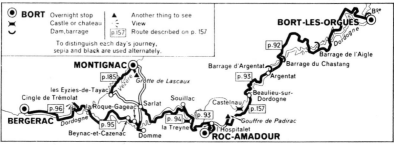

EAST–WEST CROSS-COUNTRY PROGRAMME

From Bort-les-Orgues to Bergerac (3 days—272 miles)

BORT-LES ORGUES	Bort-les-Orgues–Roc-Amadour or vice versa	BORT-LES ORGUES
	120 miles by car plus 3¼ hours sightseeing	
1st Day	The road follows the picturesque Valley of the Dordogne from Bort-les-Orgues to Castelnau.	
	The great dams that are a feature of the upper valley—the Bort** (¼ hour), the Aigle** (¼ hour) the Chastang* and the Sablier—are succeeded, first by the old houses rising one behind the other above the river bank at Argentat*, and then by the two masterpieces of the church at Beaulieu-sur-Dordogne* (½ hour) with its south doorway and Castelnau Castle** (¾ hour). The red mass of its walls and towers stands on a promontory, overlooking the confluence of the Cère and the Dordogne.	
Lunch at Argentat		Lunch at Argentat
	The Padirac Chasm*** (1½ hours) is one of the wonders of the underground world.	**3rd Day**
2nd Day	Roc-Amadour–Montignac or vice versa	
	58 miles by car plus 4½ hours sightseeing	
	Adding to the interest of the day's run across the limestone plateau and along the Valley of the Dordogne are the sightseeing opportunities to be found at Roc-Amadour*** (2½ hours), an ancient pilgrimage town built into the cliff-face, at Treyne Château* (½ hour) with its valuable furnishings, at Souillac** (½ hour) where there are fine Romanesque carvings in the church, at Sarlat** (1 hour) where there is an interesting old quarter and at Lascaux*** with its caves decorated with unique prehistoric paintings (*tours temporarily suspended*).	
Lunch at Souillac		Lunch at Souillac
		2nd Day
3rd Day	Montignac–Bergerac or vice versa	
	94 miles by car plus 4½ hours sightseeing	
	The last day of the tour is spent in the heart of the Périgord countryside and brings the tourist to the most beautiful settings in the Vézère and Dordogne Valleys: Les Eyzies-de-Tayac** (2 hours) which, since the discovery of its many prehistoric shelters and deposits, may be considered the capital of pre-history; Roque-Gageac** (½ hour) picturesquely clinging to a cliff-face above the Dordogne; Domme* (1½ hours) an ancient *bastide* and Beynac-et-Cazenac** (½ hour) overlooked by its castle.	
Lunch at Sarlat		Lunch at Sarlat
		1st Day
BERGERAC	Beyond Trémolat, a tourist road enables one to see the Trémolat ring of water**, formed by a great loop in the river.	**BERGERAC**

33

Figure 6.2. Standardised experiences of places for tourists: A journey plan from the *Guide Michelin* for Perigord (key: *** worth the trip; ** worth a detour; * of interest); the beach at Spotorno, Italian Riviera (right).

"They hardly notice the character of their surroundings ... . They do not experience the place" (Rasmussen, 1964, p.16).

the machinery and paraphenalia of travel often becomes an object of
fascination in itself.   In short, where someone goes is less important than
the act and style of going, and the tourist travels with no real sense of
either place, or past, or future, just as Cardinal Newman (cited in Hoggart,
1959, p.159) foresaw:

> "They see visions of great cities and wild regions; they are in the
> marts of commerce or amid the isles of the South; they gaze on
> Pompey's pillar or on the Andes; and nothing which meets them
> carries them either forward or backward, to any idea beyond itself.
> Nothing has a drift or a relation; nothing has a history or a promise.
> Everything stands by itself, and comes and goes in its turn, like the
> shifting scenes of a show, which leaves the spectator where he was."

6.2.2 Technique and planning

Whereas an unselfconscious and inauthentic attitude to place is associated
with mass value and kitsch, selfconscious inauthenticity tends to be
expressed in the application to places of *technique*, especially through
various forms of planning.   Much physical and social planning is founded
on an implicit assumption that space is uniform and objects and activities
can be manipulated and freely located within it; differentiation by
significance is of little importance and places are reduced to simple
locations with their greatest quality being development potential.   This
entire attitude is expressed by Richard Morrill (1970, p.20): "If there is
an underlying attitude in human geography it is that man and society try
to organise space efficiently, to locate activities and to use land in the
'best' way"; it is but a short jump from this to the idea that a major aim

of planning is to overcome spatial incongruities and inefficiencies (Abler
et al., 1971). There is little scope in this for treating places as centres of
existential significance, or even in terms of their qualities of appearance—
rather such approaches require the use of quantitative techniques of analysis
and manipulation based on the averages of economic man and a dispassionate
and impersonal approach to both place and people (figure 6.3).

Walter Gropius (1943, p.155) wrote that:

> "The majority of citizens of a specific country have similar dwelling
> and living requirements; it is therefore hard to understand why the
> dwellings we build should not show a similar unification as, say, our
> clothes, shoes or automobiles."

This simple expression of the 'machine to live in' notion, overlooking as it
does variations in requirements or the manner in which those needs are
determined and should be satisfied, can easily be applied to subdivisions
and even entire cities. What it means is that the planner or developer can,

		Variables										
		Climate	Air	Water	Solid wastes	Noise	Intake	Safety	Privacy	Number	Density	Duration	Frequency
	Home												
	School												
	Shopping												
	Commuting												
Functions	Work												
	Recreation (spirit)												
	Leisure and recreation												
	Experiences of nature												
	Healing												

Figure 6.3. Planning for places?—A technological functions matrix (from Ewald,
1967, p.281).

Having obtained 'meaningful combinations' of the controllable variables by using
principal components analysis, it is possible to relate functions to variables by means
of this matrix.

using his battery of principles and techniques, proceed to create places in a way that is quite divorced from how he experiences them; their creation is achieved objectively and through mass-production, while his experiences are direct and individual. In this way he can plan a new expressway network or a slum redevelopment scheme with the same degree of detachment "... because any empathetic feeling he may have possessed is lost outside the scope of the tunnel vision forced upon him by his methodology" (Pawley, 1971, p.92).

The reasoning which apparently lies behind this type of planning, and indeed much social and behavioural science, has been ably summarised and criticised by Noam Chomsky. He writes (1969, pp.57-58):

"One might construct some such chain of association as this. Science, as everyone knows, is responsible, moderate, unsentimental and otherwise good. Behavioural science tells us that we can be concerned only with behaviour and the control of behaviour; and it is responsible, moderate, unsentimental and otherwise good to control behaviour by appropriately applied reward and punishment. Concern for loyalties and attitudes is emotional and unscientific. As rational men, believers in the scientific ethic, we should be concerned with manipulating behaviour in a desirable direction and not be deluded by mystical notions of freedom, individual needs and free will."

This is, of course, intended as parody, but what is disturbing is that it emerges as only a slight exaggeration; such narrow and scientistic attitudes, conveniently subsuming ethical questions, are the basis for improving the efficiency of Pacification programmes in South Vietnam, for displacing single family residences by high-rise offices in the interests of economic growth, or for flooding Indian lands for the construction of hydroelectric projects. The places affected are really quite incidental so long as the specific goal is achieved with a satisfactory level of efficiency. The narrowness of such an approach, the emphasis on the abstract, economic, public interest, rather than on individual or community life and values, is profoundly inauthentic. This is indeed *technique*-dominated planning, divorced from places as we know and experience them in our everyday lives, and quite casually ignoring or obliterating them.

Perhaps Wittgenstein (cited in Passmore, 1968, p.472) was overstating his case when he wrote that "when all possible scientific questions have been answered, the problems of life remain completely untouched", but in general it does appear that the problems and methods of science are of limited value in dealing with the issues of the lived-world. Certainly in the context of place it is clear that quasi-scientific planning and social engineering need to be used with the greatest possible sensitivity. Such sensitivity is not widely apparent in most of the planning that affects places—indeed such planning appears not only to be based on an inauthentic sense of place but generally to involve no sense of place at all.

6.3 Placelessness

An inauthentic attitude towards places is transmitted through a number of
processes, or perhaps more accurately 'media', which directly or indirectly
encourage 'placelessness', that is, a weakening of the identity of places to the
point where they not only look alike but feel alike and offer the same bland
possibilities for experience. These media include mass communications,
mass culture, big business, powerful central authority, and the economic
system which embraces all these. Clearly these are neither wholly
differentiated as media nor in terms of their effects, for they are all in
some way associated with the values of kitsch and *technique*; rather they
are distinguishable cores which interlink, combine, and complement each
other both in creating landscapes which are visually and experientially
similar, and in destroying existing places. In themselves these are not
necessarily placeless, nor do we yet live in a world that is geographically
undifferentiated. What is important is that these are powerful processes of
landscape modification which do little or nothing to create and maintain
significant and diverse places.

6.3.1 Mass communication

"The old road", writes Todd Snow (1967, p.15), "was a definite place, a
strip of land that went between other places." It was a road which had to
be travelled slowly and which thus encouraged social contact as well as
involving the traveller directly in the landscape. "Since the old road was
basically an extension of a place it partook of the nature of all places and
was related to the geography beside the road as well as that of and at the
end of the road." In contrast to this is the New Road (figure 6.4), an
essentially twentieth century creation and an extension of man's vehicle;
it does not connect places nor does it link with the surrounding landscape.
"The New Road generally seems to go between cities, but the primary
requirement is that it start from where the people are and go on indefinitely,
not that it go between places or lead to places. The old road started from
and led to the city. The New Road starts everywhere and leads nowhere."
(Snow, 1967, p.14). The New Road is, of course, not alone in this, and
Briggs (1968, p.92) has written: "Before the building of great highways
tore into the heart of our cities and introduced a new placeless geography
the railways were ... destroying the sense of place."

Roads, railways, airports, cutting across or imposed on the landscape
rather than developing with it, are not only features of placelessness in
their own right, but, by making possible the mass movement of people
with all their fashions and habits, have encouraged the spread of
placelessness well beyond their immediate impacts. In 1887 Frederic
Harrison (cited in Briggs, 1968, p.86) complained that "in things spiritual
and temporal alike our modern mania is to carry with us our own way of
life, instead of accepting that which we find on the spot ... . We go

Figure 6.4. The old road and the new road: Erindale, Ontario, 1904 (courtesy of Hammond Collection, Public Archives of Ontario), and the interchange of Highways 401 and 427 under construction, Toronto.

"The old road was an extension of a place ... and was related to the geography beside the road" (Snow, 1967, p.14).

"The building of great highways ... introduced a new placeless geography" (Briggs, 1968, p.92).

abroad but we travel no longer." And this was written at the very beginning of the age of mass travel, an age in which tourism has increasingly imposed its own values and forms on all the places that have merited its attention.

Communication by transportation is only one form of communication, and the various media for the transmission of ideas—newspapers, journals, radio, television—have also had an immense, if less explicit impact on places. They have reduced the need for face-to-face contact, freed communities from their geographical constraints, and hence reduced the significance of place-based communities (Webber, 1964). They have made it possible to treat problems as widespread and general rather than local and specific, and hence to propose general solutions according to the place-free dictates of current social science and planning. This is clear, for example, in the spread of the picturesque, curvilinear street patterns in suburban areas, or in current International Style architecture with its functional and efficient use of concrete, steel, and glass. But the role of mass media is nowhere more apparent than in the environment of mass culture. Wagner (1972, p.57) writes:

> "The flood of extrinsic artifacts and continuous exotic communications has become so great that it seems almost as if 'locality' has lost its meaning. Standardizing agencies now operate more effectively and widely than at any other time in history ... . The public heed homogenized communications, thanks to the electronic media, in a way they previously never could. America is a city and Canada struggles not to be its suburb."

In short, mass communication appears to result in a growing uniformity of landscape and a lessening diversity of places by encouraging and transmitting general and standardised tastes and fashions[10].

6.3.2 Mass culture

Inevitably linked with the mass movement of people and ideas is a culture of mass values. In "masscult" fashions and designs come from above to the people, that is to say, they are formulated by manufacturers, governments, and professional designers, and are guided and communicated through mass media. They are not developed and formulated by the people themselves. Uniform products and places are created for people of supposedly uniform needs and tastes, or perhaps vice versa. "What is wanted", suggests Asa Briggs (1968, p.92), "is not to be different but to be the same." This is nowhere more clearly illustrated than in the

---

[10] Uniformity is further encouraged by the fact that such media are directed at 'average' people and are essentially one-way and provide ready-made attitudes. It is, however, possible that different media create different landscapes—this is certainly the implication of the discussions of communication by Harold Innis (1951) and Marshall McCluhan (1964).

landscapes of tourism and subtopia, and particularly in the 'other-directed' places that result from 'disneyfication', 'museumisation' and 'futurisation'.

Other-directed places. The physical impact of tourism on recipient landscapes is considerable. Garret Eckbo (1969, p.29) summarises them:

> "... tour buses; tourist hotels (from cheap to elegant); the commercial seductions called 'souvenirs'; entertainments ranging in style and appeal from pinball arcades, through Las Vegas-type gambling and show business, to art and history museums; recreational resorts, again existing in a dazzling range from camping in national parks to luxurious idling in plush hotels set in handsome natural settings in the mountains or by lakes or oceans."

Tourism is an homogenizing influence and its effects everywhere seem to be the same—the destruction of the local and regional landscape that very often initiated the tourism, and its replacement by conventional tourist architecture and synthetic landscapes and pseudo-places. Mishan (1967, p.104) claims that "the tourist trade, in a competitive scramble to uncover all places of once quiet repose, of wonder, beauty and historic interest to the money-flushed multitude, is in effect literally and irrevocably destroying them". And Sissman (1971, p.34) gives a specific example—"the Majorca culture has virtually been effaced by miles and miles of high-rise condominiums, discotheques and souvenir stands". He could just as easily have cited the Mediterranean coasts of France, Spain, or Italy; and these, of course, now differ only marginally from the touristscapes of Miami or Waikiki (figure 6.5).

The landscapes of tourism are typified by what J. B. Jackson (1970, pp.64–65) has called 'other-directed architecture'—that is, architecture which is deliberately directed towards outsiders, spectators, passers-by, and above all consumers. The total effect of such architecture is the creation of other-directed places which suggest almost nothing of the people living and working in them, but declare themselves unequivocally to be "Vacationland" or "Consumerland" through the use of exotic decoration, gaudy colours, grotesque adornments, and the indiscriminate borrowing of styles and names from the most popular places of the world (figures 6.6 and 6.7). In 1849 John Ruskin (n.d., chapter IV, section 19, pp.115–116) wrote of London:

> "... how is it that the tradesmen cannot understand that custom is to be had only by selling good tea and cheese and cloth, and that people come to them for their honesty, and their readiness, and their right wares, and not because they have Greek cornices over their windows, or their names in huge gilt letters on their house front?... How much better for them it would be—how much happier, how much wiser, to put their trust upon their own truth and industry, and not on the idiocy of the consumer."

Figure 6.5. Landscapes of tourism: International style hotels, condominiums and holiday apartments at Waikiki, Hawaii, and La Grande Motte, South France, and the point of embarkation for a memorial boat tour of Canoe Lake in Algonquin Park, the lake in which the Canadian landscape painter Tom Thomson was drowned.

"The tourist trade, in a competitive scramble to uncover all places of wonder, beauty and historic interest, is in effect literally and irrevocably destroying them" (Mishan, 1967, p.104).

His advice has not only not been heeded, but the 'idiocy of the consumer' is precisely the thing in which trust has been placed by advertisers and retailers. Kitschy, other-directed places are the rule in downtown shopping and entertainment districts (where they reach perhaps their purest expression in the cityscape of pornography or 'pornscape'), in the roadside strips which fringe most cities, and in almost all tourist centres.

Disneyfication. Possibly the apogee of other-directed places is to be found in 'Super Colossal Amusement Parks' (Greer, 1974), whether fantastic Disneylands, idealised Historylands or futurist Expositions. The products of 'disneyfication' are absurd, synthetic places made up of a surrealistic combination of history, myth, reality and fantasy that have little relationship with particular geographical setting (figure 6.8):

> "Disney World is a world without violence, confrontation, ideological or racial clashes, without politics ... . It is a world that is white, Anglo-Saxon and Puritan Protestant, often red-neck, void of ethnic cast ... . Once you leave the America of Frontierland and Liberty Square to wander through the Magic Kingdom to Fantasyland, you enter a realm which is vaguely imitation English or pseudo-European ... . Off to Tomorrowland and it's back to America ... . Adventureland is one of those places you've seen a hundred times in old Grade B movies ... In the not too distant tomorrow you'll be able, if you're rich or corporate enough, not only to visit Disney World but to live there in a completely planned and auto-less city tentatively being called the Experimental Prototype Community of Tomorrow" (Ferritti, 1973).

Figure 6.6. Other direction in places (A): "Conspicuous facades, exotic decoration and landscaping, a lavish use of lights and colours and signs ..." (Jackson, 1970, p.68).

A pineapple car hire office, Honolulu; a roadside store, Vermont; the pornscape of the Barbary Coast, San Francisco; Honest Ed's Department Store, Toronto.

In short, Disney World and its equivalents offer the best of imagined and plastic history and adventure from the world over, and combine this either implicitly or explicitly with a vision of a technological utopia.

It is easy to dismiss these fantasy pseudo-places as being just for family fun, and as being isolated and of limited numbers (there are probably fewer than thirty large-scale Amusement Parks in the United States, and few elsewhere), but this would miss much of their significance. That they are not intended solely for children is indicated by the following account of what is perhaps the most remarkable fantasy place yet conceived— Biblelands in southeastern Ohio:

> "Inspired by the success of Disneyland, a group of religious-minded men is planning a $30 million Biblelands—complete with camel rides, fishing in the Sea of Galilee and side trips to the land of milk and honey ... . 'With the pressures that are on man today we need a kind of recreational area that does more than just recreate, we need inspiration', says Biblelands' director of production ..." (Biblelands, 1972).

These fantasylands are in part places of escaping from drab, corrupt, inefficient reality; they are also places of inspiration in which everyone is nice and everyone smiles. But in addition they appear to be to some extent utopias made real which provide *guaranteed* excitement, amusement, or interest, while eliminating the effort and chance of travel or imagination.

Figure 6.7. Other direction in places (B): "... and an indiscriminate borrowing and imitating to produce certain pleasing effects" (Jackson, 1970, p.68).

Craigleith ski village, Ontario—Ersatz Swiss style cottages in a Canadian setting with rebuilt log cabins; a 'hummer' house (No. 533 Spadina Road, Toronto)—an electricity substation masquerading as a neo-Georgian single-family house; Portmeirion, North Wales—a village collected by the architect Clough Williams Ellis in the early 20th century incorporating buildings from all over the world—Burmese temple dancers, Welsh cottages, fake Italian churches.

And as utopias they provide ideals to be copies; the Experimental Prototype Community of Tomorrow indicates the way in which things should be done in the outside world (there is at least one North American educational television programme that uses Disney World to show how city problems of transportation, servicing, etc. can be solved). There would, of course, be difficulties in any attempt to copy the techniques of Disney World: not only is it an instant, historyless development, but it is also in effect a small totalitarian state.

The grand amusement parks are the most spectacular and obvious manifestations of a much wider process of disneyfication. The mixing of fantasy and reality is apparent in the exotic architecture of Ali Baba or Chinese restaurants, in plywood cutout pigs holding menus outside French cafés, in little plaster gnomes and elves ornamenting gardens. Disneyfication is in fact not a limited and superficial phenomenon that is incidental to the main theme of contemporary western culture. Rather it appears, on one level, to be a popular and kitschy expression of belief in the objective mastery of nature and of change: monsters and history and wild animals are brought safely under control. And on another deeper level disneyfication seems to be one particular and unselfconscious expression of the attitudes lying behind the technical achievement that made such mastery possible. George Grant (1969, p.15) writes:

"This achievement is not something simply external to us, as so many people envision it. It is not merely an external environment which we make and choose as we want—a playground in which we are able to do more and more, an orchard where we can always pick variegated fruit.

Figure 6.8. Disneyfication: The Big Nickel, Sudbury—fantastic money; assorted dwarfs and gnomes for personal disneyfication; and Champlain Storyland, Ontario (right).

"This achievement is not something simply external to us ... . It moulds us in what we are, in our actions and thoughts and imaginings" (Grant, 1969, p.15).

It moulds us in what we are ... in our actions and thoughts and imaginings. Its pursuit has become our dominant activity and that dominance fashions both the public and private realms."

Museumisation. A particular form of disneyfication is the preservation, reconstruction and idealisation of history, or "museumisation". The manifestations of this process are reconstituted pioneer villages, restored castles and reconstructed forts (figure 6.9). Museumised places are almost inevitably made suitably tidy and bowdlerised to correspond with "the dream image of an immutable past" (Whitehill, cited in Lowenthal, 1968, p.81), and Sissman (1971, p.34) has written of the United States that "Regional differences are stylised into the cute and kitschy tourist attraction—the Colonial South is embalmed at Williamsburg and Colonial New England in Sturbridge Village." Such places strive for accuracy of replication in their visible detail, but so long as they meet the general demand for historical atmosphere it does not seem to matter whether they are genuine relics or complete fakes and facades. The brochure (St. Lawrence Parks Commission, n.d.) for Upper Canada Village, one of the more elaborate cases of museumisation in Canada, declares:

> "Here you find the gentle life of *typical early Canadian villages*, as they existed during the first years of the last century. All of the forty or more buildings—homes, churches, mills, taverns, shops—*have been relocated in the village* from their original sites in the St. Lawrence Valley, and all have been restored or refurbished with painstaking accuracy and devoted attention to detail" (my emphases).

Figure 6.9. Museumisation: Fort Mackinaw, Michigan and a relocated, reconstructed log house at Craigleith, Ontario.

"Restoration ... the most total destruction a building can suffer ... . And as for direct and simple copying, it is palpably impossible" (Ruskin, n.d., pp.184–185).

Clearly this is not a 'typical' village, but a quite contrived development made in accordance with our romantic images of the past and using the best examples of buildings available.

Such a blasé attitude to historical accuracy is not always apparent in museumisation, and sometimes an attempt is made to recreate the past in its totality. Of the new Iron Age village of Lejre in Denmark we read: "This is a place where you can not only look at the past—you can live in it." If you are in good health you can apply to live three thousand years ago:

"The Prehistoric Village is one of the rare places on earth where individuals may learn first-hand what it was like to ride a horse, catch sheep, wield an axe, cook food in baked clay pots in a prehistoric furnace, spin thread and survive—that's the big word, survive—over a period of time with no modern conveniences." (Libby, 1975, p.G1)

This establishes a new pace for museumisation and perhaps in a few years we will be able to choose not where, but when in the plastic past we wish to go for our holiday.

For those with a discerning sense of place the historical atmosphere or even educational value of such villages may not be enough—Ian Nairn (1965, p.5) writes of the "nemesis of Old Sturbridge" and declares unequivocally that "no identity is better than a false identity". But the most withering comment of all is John Ruskin's (n.d., pp.184–185):

"Neither by the public, nor by those who have the care of public monuments, is the true meaning of the word *restoration* understood. It means the most total destruction a building can suffer: a destruction out of which no remnants can be gathered: a destruction accompanied by a false description of the thing destroyed ... . And as for direct and simple copying, it is palpably impossible ... . There was yet in the old *some* life, some mysterious suggestion of what it had been, and of what it had lost; some sweetness in the gentle lines which rain and sun had wrought. There can be none in the brute hardness of the new carving."

Futurisation. Allied with museumisation, but looking ahead and not to the past, and more earnest and deliberate than disneyfication, is 'futurisation'—the selfconscious making of futuristic landscapes and places. This is done most spectacularly at great international exhibitions, though it is apparent in any design that attempts to be innovative and ahead of its time. The aim of international expositions has been stated rather mundanely by the International Exhibitions Board as the presentation of the technology of the world while stressing its value and usefulness (New York Times, 1967, p.10); but that more than this is involved is apparent in the promoters' description of Expo 67 in Montreal as "the greatest, most imaginative world exhibition of them all, bringing you the sights and

Figure 6.10. Futurisation: Ontario Place, Toronto—an amusement and exhibition centre in the style of an Archigram walking city; and innovative exurban houses near Toronto.

sounds, the hopes and dreams of more than two thirds of all the nations
on earth" (New York Times, 1967, p.3). Such exhibitions are expressions
of faith in progress, technological utopias in which all nations are united
in a setting that combines the best utilitarian design and most imaginative
futurist design.

These creations of architects speculating freely about the nature of cities
two or three decades hence [the Ontario Place recreation/exhibition
complex in Toronto combines a geodesic dome with pods and elevated
walkways above the lake, and looks for all the world like an Archigram
montage (figure 6.10)] are deliberately intended as points of innovation,
as trend-setters in design and style and taste: they are meant to be copied.
Robert Fulford (cited in Jackson, 1973, p.99) wrote of Expo 67: "It will,
hopefully, change our cities because, after Expo, they look ugly, untidy,
even uncomfortable." But to create landscapes that are futurist,
innovative, or selfconsciously ahead of their times, whether on the grand
scale of world exhibitions or on the small scale of an individual 'modernist'
house or office building, is to make environments which are founded on
the standardising principles of technology and hence are truly 'International'
and placeless. But futurisation is a remarkable form of placelessness, for,
by looking continually ahead for styles and techniques that are new, it is
also continually destructive of place, denying even the degree of authenticity
that time and tradition might lend to places.

Subtopia. Translated into the everyday landscapes of suburbia and urban
fringe areas other-direction, commercialisation and disneyfication constitute
what Ian Nairn (1965, p.7) has called 'subtopia', or the "mindless mixing
up of all man-made objects without any pattern of purpose or relationship".
Subtopia is starkly illustrated in its American forms in Peter Blake's
photographic study—*God's Own Junkyard* (1964). In part it comprises
endless subdivisions of identical houses; Coles and Erikson (1971, p.100)
describe the suburbia of a Middle American housewife "with its ranch
houses, mile after mile, to the point that one remembers how to get to a
particular house this way: take the fourth right after the shopping centre,
then the third left, then the second right, then the first left, then count five
houses on the right. ("I have to be careful *myself*", she said, "one wrong
turn and I'm lost. The houses were all built by the same company.")"
Subtopia also consists of commercial strip developments with their
confusion of wire and colour and signs and cars and parking lots; and of
shopping plazas such as the one on the outskirts of Toronto described by

Figure 6.11. (see over). Subtopia: Suburban Brussels, Calgary, Toronto; a belated
town centre, Mississauga, Ontario; council houses in Tredegar, South Wales; suburban
apartments at Evreux, North France.

"The mindless mixing up of all man-made objects without any pattern of purpose
or relationship and the propagation of lack of identity" (Nairn, 1965, p.7).

Ian Young (1969, pp.86–87):

"A flat, stark, one-storey building constructed of several huge rectangles of glass and chalkbrick, splayed across the centre of a vast, empty carpark. A few neon signs shine meaninglessly from the walls, and on the smooth black lot the white parking lines look like cryptic glyphs of gigantic proportions; at intervals between them are high white metal poles, each with two lozenge-shaped bottle-green lamps suffusing the whole area in a ghastly green light. On each of the poles a chain clangs monotonously, metal against metal, as the wind blows across the empty lot. The lifelessness, the chilling stillness, conveys nothing human at all. It seems like nothing so much as a Martian landscape—the first scientific laboratory on the barren surface of a cold, alien planet."

In other countries subtopia may take slightly different forms—in England the houses are semidetached, the signs more subdued, there are

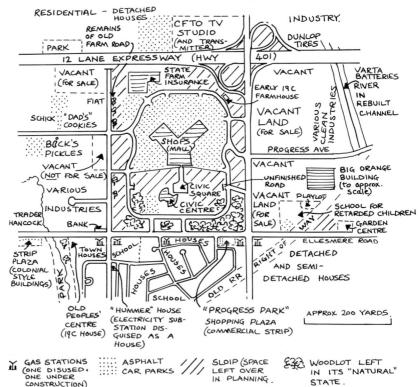

Figure 6.12. Subtopia: A deliberately untidy map of an accidentally confused landscape. The Scarborough town centre indoor shopping mall and Scarborough civic centre constitute the geographical, retailing, and administrative heart of Scarborough. a suburban borough of Metropolitan Toronto. They have little relationship with the surrounding land uses, which in turn have little relationship with each other.

fewer plazas; in France there are blocks of virtually identical public housing apartments around every town (figure 6.11). But the effects are much the same everywhere—it becomes virtually impossible to tell one locality from another, for they all look alike and feel alike; there is little spatial ordering that can be experienced directly (except perhaps from a car), for subtopia has been developed not on the basis of direct experience but in an *ad hoc* way from the remote and abstract perspective of maps and plans; residential areas are bisected by power lines and highways, residential streets run abruptly into shopping centres standing in the middle of parking lots and left over space, and town centres appear to be a peripheral afterthought (figure 6.12). In short, subtopia describes a set of apparently randomly located points and areas, each of which serves a single purpose and each of which is isolated from its setting, linked only by roads which are themselves isolated from the surrounding townscape except for the adjacent strips of other-directed buildings.

6.3.3 Big business

To a very great extent the landscapes of tourism and subtopia are consequences of the activities of big business, for they are inevitably made up of the products and reflect the needs dictated by such business even when they have not been constructed directly by them. In creating products for profit it seems that places merit little concern, whether in the production, management, or retailing of those products, or in their use in the landscape (figure 6.13).

Before the nineteenth century most industries and businesses were local and small concerns, and this was reflected in the way in which they generally fitted into their particular settings, were made from local building materials and were in scale with their environment. The industrial revolution brought with it a standardisation and gigantism that was both potentially and actually damaging to places. When Yi-fu Tuan (1969, p.203) remarks that the new urban landscapes of China have a certain sameness about them because they were all built in haste and are all responses to an industrial revolution, he could also have included much of Europe and North America. Steel mills, oil refineries, light engineering works, quarries, waste disposal sites, all have an appearance that is quite independent of location. Furthermore the sheer scale of modern mining, manufacturing, and business enterprises tends to obliterate places, whether through flooding by dam construction, digging them up for minerals, burying them beneath slag heaps, or simply building over them[11].

[11] An extreme form of such place destruction that has received very little attention is the deliberate destruction of places in war. While this has a history as long as that of warfare itself, it has recently, as R. J. Lifton (1967) has noted, moved into a new quantitative and qualitative dimension—places can be obliterated while maintaining a casual air of detachment. This is apparent both in the bombings of London, Dresden, and Hiroshima in the Second World War, and in the electronic war in Vietnam.

(A) Abbauten—kaolin mines, Cornwall; nickel mine, Falconbridge, Ontario.

Figure 6.13. The placeless landscapes of industry.

"With these, and the world spreading factories, he interlinks all geography, all lands" (Walt Whitman, *Years of the Modern,* p.339).

(B) Manufacturing—steelworks, Hamilton, Ontario; chemical works, Thionville.

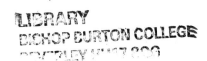

(C) Retailing—Kentucky Fried Chicken; Howard Johnson's, anywhere.

(D) Administration—Downtown Toronto from without and within.

Mumford (1961, pp.450–452) has a term for this sort of destruction—
Abbau, or unbuilding. Such destruction is not merely placeless in that it
perpetrates uniformity and disorder, but it is explicitly anti-place as well.
   The increasing similarity and grand scale of operation apply not just to
the mining and manufacturing centres but also to the associated
management and retailing centres. It is above all the offices of large
companies that constitute the developments in city centres, and these are
uniformly in the placeless style of International architecture. Skyscrapers
can, of course, give distinctive profiles to cities when viewed from a
distance, as for instance New York; but from within they create "wells of
stone and steel" (Camus, 1959, p.70) that offer few clues to the identity
of any particular city. Likewise the retail outlets of companies assume
similar characteristics everywhere—Shell, Esso, Holiday Inns, Coca Cola
advertisements, and all the other visual forms of international business
provide reassurance to the confused and weary traveller. In an excellent
analysis of Howard Johnson restaurants Stephen Kurtz (1973, p.20)
observes that "every Howard Johnson's looks so much like every other
that it is nearly impossible to tell, from the restaurant alone, whether one
is in Maine or Kansas, in California or the Carolinas". The reasons for this
sameness do not lie simply in economic and practical concerns; Kurtz
suggests that this uniformity is an attempt to replace "the infinity of
westward expansion with that of circularity". Be this as it may, it is
certainly the case that Howard Johnson's, like most other mass-production
companies, has created settings for their products which appeal to instincts
of tradition, morality, and home that cannot be denied. Kurtz continues:
"The genius of Hojo's, of course, lies in its conscious pastiche of
everything that is cosy and traditional—church spires, town halls and
cottages—to perform a thoroughly modern function ... Hojo's preserves the
'home from home' tradition by using the same nostalgic decorative devices
favoured by the suburban homeowners who are its chief patrons."
   Whether in advertising, packaging, or the product itself, there is very
little that companies involved in mass production leave to chance.
Everything is carefully designed and deliberately contrived to aid in the
selling of the product, and this involves both a response to mass culture
and an attempt to maintain and create such a culture by dictating uniform
tastes and fashions. And with a relatively small number of international
cartels operating on an ever larger scale it is clear that the only possible
consequence is a growing standardisation in the cultural landscapes of the
world, both at the points of production and administration, and at the
points of consumption.

6.3.4 Central authority
As big business has replaced small businesses in the last two hundred years,
so centralised government has replaced local initiative. In fact even when
the state is not actively consuming the products of private industry, it

functions very much as a big business in such areas as public housing and
resource management. Galbraith (1967, p.305) has observed that "the
line between public and private authority in the industrial system is
indistinct and in large measure imaginary". And although the state
exercises its authority through legislation, and business power lies in the
control of consumer preference, the result in terms of landscape is much
the same—namely standardisation and uniformity. "Central authority",
wrote Whittlesey (1935, p.90), "undertakes to act for the whole of its
territory in specified matters. This tends to produce uniformity in
cultural impress even where the natural landscape is diverse". This is
clear in the nationwide use of standard models for public housing, road
bridges, rustic log-cabins in National Parks, and less obviously in the
application of national ordinances, controls on development and legislation
which directly or indirectly affect land use practices.

With considerable control over economic expansion and physical
planning the capacity of the state and the lower levels of government for
place-making or place destruction is immense. That this capability is
being used largely for furthering various forms of placelessness is a
reflection partly of the fact that increasingly authority has passed to the
more central and remote levels of government. Over a century ago Alexis
de Tocqueville (1945, II, pp.312–313) argued that democracy would lead
to a centralisation of power and that "... every central government worships
uniformity; uniformity relieves it from inquiry into an infinity of details,
which must be attended to if rules have to be adapted to different men,
instead of indiscriminately subjecting all men to the same rule". Perhaps
then uniformity and placelessness are inevitable consequences of the
American form of democracy. But it must also be recognised that the
state is as subservient as all other parts of modern society to *technique*
and the economic-industrial system, and they too are in no small way
responsible for placelessness.

6.3.5 The economic system

Both large corporations and governments are operating within and
perpetuating an economic and industrial system, and whether we consider
this to be a controlled and manipulated thing or a more or less self-
regulating market, there is no question that it pervades all aspects of
modern life. Economics is not just a matter of production, distribution,
and consumption, but a complete way of life that even takes on the
character of a religion with regular financial reports on national television
news attended to uncomprehendingly but faithfully by a multitude of
devotees. Jacques Ellul (1967, p.219) has written: "Economic *technique*
does not encounter man in textbooks but in the flesh ... . The human
being is changing slowly under the pressure of the economic milieu; he is
in the process of becoming the uncomplicated being the liberal economist
constructed." And that uncomplicated being is one whose needs are

collectivised by publicity, by standardisation of goods and by intellectual uniformity (p.175). Such collectivisation in association with increasing control over markets enables the achievement of the primary goals of efficient operation, profit maximisation, and corporate growth and survival (Galbraith, 1967). There can be little scope in all this for matters of quality or for the needs and subtleties of individual people or particular places. Both of these must be organised so that they correspond more closely with what is believed to be efficient.

Richard Morrill (1970, p.202) concludes his textbook on *The Spatial Organisation of Society* with a discussion of any one of the 'poorer nations':

"If the chosen strategy of investment is successful, developments will spread from the growth centres to their hinterlands until all the territory is brought into a unified economy. Such an orderly development should lead to more even distribution of population, production and income and perhaps even a closer approximation to the theoretical landscape ... than is presently true of most advanced countries."

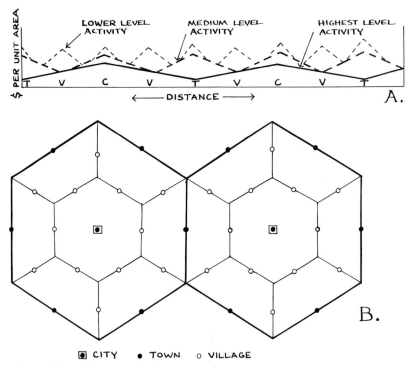

Figure 6.14. A theoretical landscape:
(A) Traverse across a central-place landscape (from Morrill, 1970, p.68).
(B) The corresponding spatial structure of a central-place landscape.

"When all possible scientific questions have been answered, the problems of life remain completely untouched" (Wittgenstein, cited in Passmore, 1968, p.472).

Here it appears that the abstractions of economic theory have become guidelines for the way in which society and landscape should develop and be organised (figure 6.14). Sense of place and attachment to place are not merely unimportant, but their very absence is an economic virtue and placelessness is to be sought after for it makes possible the attainment of greater levels of spatial efficiency. However attractive such landscapes may be theoretically, in experience they are rarely so pleasant. Henry James (1968, pp.463–464) was referring to the railroad in America, but he could have been writing of the impact of *technique* and economic efficiency anywhere, when he wrote:

> "You touch this great lonely land ... only to plant upon it some ugliness ... . You convert the large and noble sanities that I see around me, you convert them one after another to crudities, to invalidities, hideous and unashamed ... . This is the meaning surely of the inveterate rule that you multiply and develop to the perpetrations you call 'places'."

6.4 The components of a placeless geography

All formal, scientific geography that is concerned with the relative location and description of phenomena and regions presupposes a geography of immediate experiences of the lived-world. Such an experiential geography is differentiated into places according to our experiences of particular physical settings and landscapes and our intentions towards them. This is an authentic geography, a geography of places which are felt and understood for what they are—that is, as symbolic or functional centres of life for both individuals and communities. It is a geography that is manifest in a diversity of man-made forms and landscapes, forms which are in accord with their physical and cultural settings, which have humanness in their scale and their symbols. Above all it is a geography which is primarily the product of the efforts of insiders, those living in and committed to places, and a geography which declares itself only to those insiders or to those willing and able to experience places empathetically.

A geography that is based on wholly authentic place-experience and place-making has probably never occurred, but in many cultures less technologically sophisticated than our own a profound sense of place has certainly prevailed. The depth of meaning and diversity of places associated with such authentic experience are, however, greatly weakened in most contemporary cultures. The development and diffusion of the inauthentic attitudes to place of kitsch and *technique*, and the standardised manifestations of these attitudes in the landscape, appear to be widespread and increasing in most of the western world. The trend is towards an environment of few significant places—towards a placeless geography, a flatscape, a meaningless pattern of buildings (figure 6.15).

It is now possible to summarise the main components of such a 'placeless geography' in which different localities both look and feel alike, and in which distinctive places are experienced only through superficial and stereotyped images, and as 'indistinct and unstable' backgrounds to our social and economic roles (figure 6.16). The following listing is simply an attempt to summarise and tie together the previous discussion on placelessness and inauthentic attitudes to place, and a classification of the main characteristics of a placeless landscape.

1. Manifestations of placelessness
A. *Other-directedness in places*
Landscape made for tourists
Entertainment districts
Commercial strips
Disneyfied places ⎫
Museumised places ⎬ (Synthetic or pseudo-places)
Futurist places ⎭

B. *Uniformity and standardisation in places*
Instant new towns and suburbs
Industrial commercial developments
New roads and airports, etc
International styles in design and architecture

Figure 6.15. A placeless geography—Chicago and West Toronto.

"The richly varied places of the world are rapidly being obliterated under a meaningless pattern of buildings, monotonous and chaotic" (Moore, 1962, pp.33–34).

C. *Formlessness and lack of human scale and order in places*
Subtopias
Gigantism (skyscrapers, megalopoli)
Individual features unrelated to cultural or physical setting

D. *Place destruction (Abbau)*
Impersonal destruction in war (e.g. Hiroshima, villages in Vietnam)
Destruction by excavation, burial
Destruction by expropriation and redevelopment by outsiders (e.g. urban expansion)

E. *Impermanence and instability of places*
Places undergoing continuous redevelopment (e.g. many central business districts)
Abandoned places

The characteristics identified in this simple classification are not necessarily all-inclusive, nor are they mutually exclusive—one locality may possess several of the manifestations of placelessness. Furthermore these particular features are merely the superficial expressions of deeper processes and attitudes which encourage placelessness.

2. Media and systems transmitting placelessness
A. Mass communication and modes of diffusion of mass attitudes and fashions of
   kitsch.
B. Mass culture of dictated and standardised values; maintained by but making
   possible mass communications.
C. Big business and multi-national corporations: these encourage standardisation of
   products and needs to ensure economic survival, and they supply the objects of
   kitsch through the application of *technique*.
D. Central authorities: these encourage uniformity of places in the interests of
   efficiency and through the exercise of a uniform power.
E. The economic system: the abstract system, dominated by *technique*, which
   underlies and embraces all of the above.

These media constitute, in effect, the interrelated processes through
which placeless landscapes develop. To some extent their influence is
direct, as for example in the International Style offices of big business,
but they also are channels for the transmission and dissemination of the
fundamental attitudes that stand behind placelessness, and for their
translation into physical and visual form.

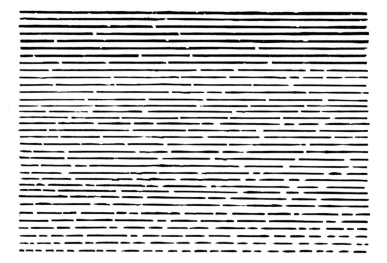

Figure 6.16. The plotting of a placeless geography: Melvin Webber's representation
of the non-place urban realm of the United States.

"Geographical space extends horizontally and level of specialization vertically ... .
The bars then represent the realms which extend in overlapping patterns across
the continent, those at the highest levels being the spatially most extensive.
Individuals participate in first one then another realm, as they play first one role
then another. The spatial patterns of realms are thus indistinct and unstable"
(Webber, 1964, p.119).

3. Inauthentic attitude to place

A. Attitudes relating to *technique*, in which places are understood to be manipulable in the public interest and are seen only in terms of their functional and technical properties and potentials.

B. Attitudes relating to kitsch, in which places are experienced and created only in terms of stereotyped, contrived, superficial and mass values.

These inauthentic attitudes to place are themselves specific forms of an inauthentic mode of existence in which both individuals and societies fail to recognise the realities and responsibilities of existence, and do not experience the world and its places for what they are. Such an inauthentic existence is the very root and essence of placelessness, and the superficial expressions that constitute placeless geographies can only be properly understood in terms of such profound inauthenticity.

Experiences of the present-day landscape

The subtle and complex relationship between place and placelessness is valuable for understanding at least one aspect of our experiences of the geographies we live in. But if place and placelessness are treated naively, as two distinct and opposed phenomena, then they can become rigid preconceptions and categories that can all too easily be imposed on particular settings. Thus there are sweeping condemnations like Osbert Lancaster's description (1959, p.186) of the 'coca-colonial' landscapes of roadside strips as "great deposits of architectural sewage", or Peter Blake's justification of his *God's Own Junkyard* (1964, p.7) as a muckraking book "because there seems to be so much muck around that needs to be raked so that this country may be made fit to live in". These are familiar criticisms that are usually combined with a simultaneous lament and plea for the local, handicraft, harmonious landscapes of peasant societies; or for the well-proportioned, ordered, and civilised landscapes of classical Greece, the Renaissance, or the eighteenth century. Grady Clay (1973, pp.23–37) calls such rigidly conditioned points of view 'fixes', for they fix attitudes towards landscape and provide ready-made prejudgements.

Negative interpretations of present-day landscapes both appeal to the widespread and probably ageless sentiment that the past must have been better than the present, and are nicely uncomplicated: past places were good, present placelessness is bad, therefore we should make places in the old way. Such a 'fix' is far too simple. Landscape is not merely an aesthetic background to life, rather it is the setting that both expresses and conditions cultural attitudes and activities, and significant modifications to landscape are not possible without major changes in social attitudes.

To grasp the overall character of placelessness it is necessary to put it into its contemporary context of the present-day landscape and to clarify the main aspects of experience of this landscape, for it is this landscape and these experiences that embrace and perhaps condition placelessness. Clearly many approaches and interpretations could contribute to this aim, and the following discussion can be no more than an introduction to and exploration of the more obvious forms of experience of present-day landscapes.

7.1 The distinctiveness of experiences of present-day landscapes
From the perspective of experience landscape cannot be understood merely as an assemblage of objects, landforms, houses, and plants. These comprise no more than a physical setting that can be grasped only in terms of a particular set of personal and cultural attitudes and intentions that give meaning to that setting. Landscapes always possess character that derives from the particular association of their physical and built characteristics with the meanings they have for those who are experiencing them; in

other words character and meaning are imputed to landscapes by the intentionality of experience. If we believe suburbia to possess "a massive monotonous ugliness" (Blake, 1964, p.17) and mountains to be spiritually uplifting, then these are probably the experiences we will have of suburban and mountain landscapes. This is not to suggest some form of idealism— the landscape often reaches out to guide our intentions and our experiences, and settings can force their monotony or their drama upon us. Landscapes are therefore always imbued with meanings that come from how and why we know them; but whereas with place this intentionality is focused and directed onto an inside that is distinct from an outside, with landscape it is diffuse and without concentration. Landscape is both the context for places and an attribute of places: there is a distinctive cultural landscape of Provence, and Roussillon is a place in Provence that partakes of that landscape and is framed by it, yet has its own distinctive townscape.

For most of the time landscape is of little or no interest to us—it is merely there as a background and context for more immediate concerns such as looking after children, writing books or whatever. Occasionally this uninterest is interrupted by casual attention to the landscape, its forms and relationships and significances. Thus when we are travelling on unfamiliar routes, visiting new towns, buying a new house, or perhaps just looking around, the appearance and character of landscapes become matters of interest. Such casual attention may provide memories or generate reflections but it makes no great impact on us and has no great depth, unless perhaps when it is repeatedly in the context of the familiar settings of our home region. Very rarely, however, casual attention may be wholly transcended by a peak experience—a particular setting because of its form or our inclinations toward it enters our consciousness in a profound way that provides an abrupt discontinuity in habitual experience. Such peak experiences of topophilia may give us a feeling of joy, ecstasy, of awe or despair, of unity with our surroundings, of perfection (cf Maslow, 1968, p.83), and although the actual experience is almost certainly brief and we lapse back into uninterest and casual interest in landscape, the impact is deep and can lead to a change in self-awareness or constitute a touchstone by which we can judge all our other experiences of landscapes.

The discontinuous nature of most experience of landscape is accompanied by 'selective vision'—we tend to see what we want to see, blanking out the ugly, the boring, the offensive, and the familiar and unchanging (Arnheim, 1969, p.19). Burchard (in Kepes, 1956, p.13) has suggested that such selectivity is practised particularly for man-made forms:

> "The desecrations of nature which we have permitted ... have taught us to be selective in our vision, probably too selective. The Rockies ... do not exact that selectivity and we find them both restful and stimulating at the same time. Thus we are ardent sightseers and travel as far as we can to have a few moments of this kind of relief."

However, selectivity is not constant but culturally determined, and mountains have not always been thought attractive and restful; before Rousseau argued that the scenery of the Alps was spiritually uplifting travellers would keep their carriage blinds drawn to avoid seeing the hideous mountains. But whatever we choose not to see, whether it is man-made or natural, the point remains that vision and attention are discriminating. There are gaps in our experiences of landscapes—settings and scenes which we effectively screen out because we do not like them or do not understand them or have no interest in them. Conversely, there may be certain forms and features which we always notice, rather like architectural historians picking out only those buildings that belong to an acknowledged architectural school or bear the mark of Le Corbusier or the Bauhaus even when they are hidden in a mass of buildings of indeterminate origin. It seems that we are able to accept without worry such biases and such lacunae in our experience of landscapes.

The architect Aldo Van Eyck (cited in Venturi, 1966, p.19) has suggested that it is unwise to harp continually on about what is different in our time to such an extent that we lose touch with what is essentially the same. Presumably landscapes have always been structured and given identity by human intentions and experiences, and have always expressed cultural attitudes and beliefs and provided the contexts for the profound and trivial needs and experiences of the people who live in them. In these respects there are important similarities between past and present consciousness of landscape; but there are also marked differences between the landscapes that are currently being created and those of previous ages. The new landscape is the distinctive product and expression of new beliefs, aesthetics, technologies and economies: God is dead or in doubt, international styles abound, machines remake geography, and massive corporations and states dominate production. Norberg-Schulz (1965, pp.168–169) has identified what is perhaps the key to these differences between present and former experience of landscapes:

> "To the peasant the rocks and the mountains are 'ugly' because he cannot cultivate them. As long as the feeling for such empirical connections was alive, man built *with* the landscape. Industrialised man, instead, believes that the technical means enable him to make everything everywhere, which implies that all empirical connections become meaningless."

There has, in brief, been a separation of man from landscape and nature. This is true in the very literal sense that we are not as close to land, sea, wind, and mountain as our ancestors, nor do we have the same involvement in creating the forms of man-made landscapes, but spend increasing amounts of time in air-conditioned, centrally-heated buildings with artificial lighting made by someone else. This separation, combined with the changes in society and economy, has had a considerable influence

on the types of environment that have been created and on the way in
which we experience landscapes. Henri Lefebvre (1971, p.38) suggests
that before the rise of competitive capitalism in the nineteenth century
even in the heart of poverty and oppression there was style, for there
were labours of skill that gave significance to the slightest object. Now
we have what he calls a "bureaucratic society of controlled consumption"
providing and maintaining an everyday world of repetitions and glossy
mass-produced objects. This society has its own landscape—a rational,
absurd, confused present-day landscape that had no equivalent prior to the
nineteenth century.

7.2 The landscape of reflection and reason

"A reflective and passionless age", wrote Kierkegaard in *The Present Age*
(1962, p.51 and p.42), "hinders and stifles all action; it levels ... it leaves
everything standing but cunningly empties it of significance". Ours is an
age of reflection in which good sense and being reasonable are admired, in
which problems are recognised, defined, analysed and resolved. The
dominant mode of thinking is rationalism, and there is no opinion, no
habit, nothing that is so firmly rooted or so widely believed that it cannot
be questioned and judged by 'reason' (Oakeshott, 1962, p.1). The origins
of this rationalism may lie in the Renaissance, but it now has a different
form; it is not a humanistic conception of man in his world but a sceptical
approach based on facts rather than thought. In this present-day
rationalism order is sought and discovered everywhere, and the mysteries
and uncertainties of experience are not accepted but are investigated and
explained. This involves a devaluation of commitment and a shift from
reliance on thought to a dependence on methods of procedure that allow
a dispassionate and objective assessment of matters. Commitment limits
options by removing the possibility of finding new, different, perhaps
better, courses of action, while careful control allows the selection between
the various options to be made in a well-considered manner. The
manifestations of noncommitment and control, of reason, pervade modern
life—they are to be found in behavioural psychology, in political
decisionmaking, in business, in urban and regional planning, in recipe
books and analyses of sexual behaviour. In all these cases knowledge is
technical: it has been reduced to sets or principles, directions and rules;
the means for success are made explicit and skill and wisdom are replaced
by mechanical procedures and expertise.

The landscape of reflection and reason is the landscape either created
directly by the application of rational, scientific techniques to particular
settings, or experienced through the adopted attitudes of rationalism.
Because there is so little skill or commitment involved, it is a strangely
passionless landscape which seems to deny deep experiences or close
attachments. The reflective landscape is ordered, sometimes blatantly and

rigidly ordered, with the lines of good sense adhered to without deviation; it is usually a landscape that has no serious concern with locality and eliminates any traces of its predecessors, for, as Oakeshott (1962, p.4) declares, "to the Rationalist, nothing is of value merely because it exists (and certainly not because it has existed for many generations), familiarity has no worth, and nothing is to be left standing for want of scrutiny". The designers of the landscapes of reflection—the developers, planners, and bureaucrats—are essentially uninvolved with such imponderable and qualitative matters as locality and history; their concern is not with the landscape as a significant setting for peoples' lives (including their own) but with the wholly reasonable aims of providing efficient and adequate housing, transportation, recreation facilities, or with making money.

The landscape of reason and reflection surrounds us. It is apparent in the theoretical and stylistic arrangements of new suburban developments, in selfconscious modern architecture, in projects for the efficient management of resources, in planned settlement patterns, in new highway systems and modern airports; but its archetypal manifestation is in new towns (figures 6.3, 6.12, 6.14, 6.15). Henri Lefebvre (1971, p.58) argues that in new towns "everyday life was cut up and laid out on the site to be put together again like the pieces of a puzzle, each piece depending on a number of organizations and institutions, each one—working life, private life, leisure—rationally exploited". In effect a lifestyle and an environment are being provided ready-made according to what the experts consider to be optimal, most efficient, most desirable, most profitable and most fashionable. In some developments the package is so complete that the houses come with appliances, carpets, sodded lawns, foundation plants, and rustic coach lamps to light the driveway.

The landscape of reflection is a public landscape, but not in the sense of J. B. Jackson (1970, "The public landscape") who uses the term to refer to the roads, monuments, and public places that give identity to communities and so enrich public existence. It is 'public' in the sense that it has been made in the public interest and for consumption by the public. Kierkegaard (1962, p.59) wrote more than a century ago that "in order that everything should be reduced to the same level it is first necessary to procure a phantom, its spirit, a monstrous abstraction, an all-embracing something which is nothing, a mirage—and that phantom is *the public*." The 'public' may indeed be a phantom, and, if it is, then so is the public landscape which has been created to supply this phantom. The public landscape nonetheless has readily identifiable features—it is levelled, for it must meet the needs of all social and economic classes; it is easily acceptable, offering little that can be judged either elevating or depressing, and little that is challenging; it is pleasant enough and comfortable; it functions adequately. But it is not a landscape that possesses any real identity of its own, nor does it foster individual or community commitment, for these may not accord with the public interest: indeed it is a landscape that is largely destitute of the moral ideals and deeply-held values that are probably necessary for such commitment to develop.

7.3 The absurd landscape

'Reflection' and 'reason' describe the landscape that is created dispassionately and without involvement; they are terms which apply both to the landscape as an object of experience and to the intentions of rational landscapemakers.   'Absurdity' however, refers primarily to the subjective experience of landscape.   Any setting, man-made or natural, rational or otherwise, can be experienced as absurd.   Albert Camus (1955, p.11) wrote: "Perceiving that the world is 'dense', sensing to what degree a stone is foreign and irreducible to us, with what intensity nature or a landscape can negate us ... that denseness and that strangeness of the world is the absurd."   Such a feeling of absurdity means that man loses his illusions, feels isolated, a stranger "deprived of the memory of a lost home or the hope of a promised land" (Camus, 1955, p.5).   It involves the sense that nothing is really clear or comprehensible, that events are beyond control and men are trapped in a web of anonymously directed and largely meaningless forces.   Absurdity is obviously oppressive, but Camus argues that, if we can accept the view of a limited universe in which nothing is possible and everything is given, we can draw strength from it, and develop an indifference to the future and a desire to live each situation to its fullest.   This is the basis for a life of acceptance in which preferences, choices, and values cease to be important.

The absurd is not some esoteric philosophical notion, but is central to life in the present age.   Robert Lifton (1969, p.38) suggests that "absurdity and mockery" have in the post-Second-World-War period become "a prominent part of a universal life style".   He finds them clearly expressed in pop art with its perfect reproductions of mass-produced objects, in the cynicism of much contemporary literature, in humour, in current slang, and increasingly in peoples' sense of themselves. Such absurdity is related to the perception of surrounding activities and beliefs as strange and inappropriate, and consequently they need not be taken seriously or accepted without being mocked.

The absurd landscape is the landscape we experience as being there, apart from us and indifferent to us.   It may be the result of our sense of absurdity, just as for Camus's outsider the division of man and setting becomes insurmountable and the absurd is everywhere.   Alternatively it may come from a feeling that there is a right way to experience landscapes to which our own experiences do not conform.   J. H. van der Berg (1965, p.206) observes that ecstatic experiences of landscapes belong to the past and that there is now a general estrangement from landscape. He writes:

> "Many of the people who, on their traditional trip to the Alps,
> ecstatically gaze at the snow of the mountain tops and at the azure of
> transparent distance, do so now out of a sense of duty ... they are
> simulating an emotion which they do not actually feel. It is simply
> not permissible to sigh at the vision of the great views and to wonder,
> for everyone to hear, whether it was really worth the trouble ... . To
> a few the landscape is still delightful. But hardly anybody feels the
> delight is so great, so overpowering, that he is moved to tears."

Whether the ecstatic experience of the landscape is a thing of the past or
not, those landscapes that we experience with simulated emotions or with
a blasé attitude of having seen it all before are indeed absurd landscapes.

There are also landscapes which can force their absurdity upon our
attention almost regardless of our predispositions. Eric Dardel (1952,
p.60) quotes the mountaineer Jean Proal: "In the zone where the rocks
and glaciers begin the mountain has lost all trace of what one might call
its humanity ... . It is not superhuman, it is ahuman. It does not reject
man, it ignores him." Such indifference comes also from man-made
landscapes: Jean Grenier discovered through the window of his room in
Sienna "an immense space where trees, skies, vines and churches whirled"
and he began to cry, "not out of delight, but from powerlessness" (cited
in Dardel, 1952, p.61). Indifference, powerlessness, the feeling that it is
all too ridiculously huge, are prompted by views of cities from the air or
even from the middle-distance isolation of a passing expressway or railway
(figures 6.1, 6.13d, 6.15). Street upon street of houses, the vast
castellations and curtain walls of modern skyscrapers in city centres, seem
not only impenetrable but monstrous as they spread out or up on a scale
that defies immediate experience. No less suggestive of absurdity are
rationally designed landscapes laid out with a mathematical precision
regardless of topography, and scenes of industrial devastation. There is
absurdity too in disneyfied landscapes of cartoon characters: bekilted
humanoid cats carrying milk jugs to advertise a chain of corner grocery
stores, Ronald MacDonald and his hamburger companions, the benign big-
brother face of Colonel Sanders staring down at us (figures 6.6, 6.8).
These are obviously ridiculous and absurd in their own right, but they are
whimsical in earnest, accepted passively if not quite unselfconsciously, and
one must presume by their continued existence that they are commercially
successful. The mass of the international-style corporate skyscrapers that
comprise the downtown core of Toronto seen from the Gardiner
Expressway is complemented by the huge billboard face of Mary—'your
girl at the Royal Bank'. The only sign of humanity, she is vast and
appropriately in scale with the skyscrapers behind her (figure 6.13d). The
soot-black sheds of the steel mills in Pittsburgh stretch almost to the horizon;
above them a billboard advertising Marlboro cigarettes shows a cowboy riding

into a multi-coloured sunset in a mountain wilderness. In such contrasts the absurdity of the present-day landscape seems to have been made almost deliberately explicit. "The absurd is laughter and comedy with a difference", writes Henri Lefebvre (1971, p.139), "it is not irony and it is not humour; here neither the situation nor the action is funny." The absurd landscape is a humourless, intensely serious, commodity that can be processed, treated, and decorated like any other commodity.

7.4 The mediating machine

Few present-day experiences of landscape are possible, and for some people no experiences are complete, without the smell of gasoline and the sound of the internal combustion engine. Yet it has become almost customary to condemn machines for divorcing us from nature and other people. "Ultimately", says Stephen Kurtz (1973, p.16), "the individual car is a symbol of Americans' desparate isolation—a vicious loneliness capable of destroying not only the rest of the world but each other as well." This is too simple. Cars, motorbikes, power boats and all those other machines for personal use have not created a rift, nor do they symbolise isolation any more than did suits of armour in the Middle Ages. On the contrary, personal machines have, in a sense, slipped into the gap that is implicit in rational and absurd experiences of landscapes. And while they appear to make manifest and may even exacerbate this separation, for instance by increasing insensitivity to the subtleties of environment, they also provide a connecting link, albeit a transitory one. Personal machines offer us new options, comforts and experiences; they also give the possibility of direct confrontations with environments and immediate participations in landscapes that reason and absurdity otherwise prevent. In the first Futurist manifesto, published in 1909, Marinetti (1972) wrote:

> "We declare that the splendour of the world has been enriched by a new beauty—the beauty of speed. A racing car with its bonnet draped with exhaust pipes like fire-breathing serpents—a roaring racing car rattling along like a machine gun is more beautiful than the winged victory of Samothrace."

The motor racetracks of the world, the care and attention lavished on cars and other machines by their owners, are testament to Marinetti's vision. Whatever the ecological arguments against powerful machines, their popularity is undeniable and the status of cars at least can scarcely be underestimated. Roland Barthes (1972, p.88) has declared:

> "I think that cars today are almost an exact equivalent of the great Gothic cathedrals: I mean the supreme creation of an era, conceived with passion by unknown artists, and consumed in image if not in usage by a whole population which expropriates them as purely magical objects."

The reasons for the popularity and status of machines are several: the freedom they offer, the convenience, the possibility of temporary escape from otherwise depressing environments (Cadillacs are surprisingly common in the poorest parts of American cities). But machines also put people in contact with the world in an exciting, immediate and challenging way. St. Exupery knew this (1940, p.67)

> "Precisely because it is perfect the machine dissembles its own existence instead of forcing itself upon our notice.
> And thus ... the realities of nature resume their pride of place. It is not with metal that the pilot is in contact. Contrary to the vulgar illusion, it is thanks to the metal, and by virtue of it that the pilot rediscovers nature ... the machine does not isolate man from the great problems of nature but plunges him more deeply into them."

Of course it is difficult to maintain that the confrontations St. Exupery experienced as a pilot in the 1920s and 1930s are comparable with those of a passenger buried inside the padded pressurised interior of a jumbo jet or in the heated, airconditioned comfort of a Buick or Mercedes. But even on the freeways of Los Angeles some excitement is there. Reyner Banham (1973, pp.216–217) claims that driving on these freeways involves "... a willing acquiescence in an incredibly demanding man/machine system ... . It demands ... an open but decisive attitude to the placing of the car on the road surface, a constant stream of decision". The experience is complete: "As you acquire the special skills involved, the Los Angeles freeways become a special way of being alive", and the drivers are united with their highway environment. "Their white-wall tyres are singing over the diamond-cut, antiskid grooves in the concrete road surface, the selector levers of their automatic gearboxes are firmly in DRIVE, and their radio is on."

The excitement of driving must be known to almost everyone who has driven a machine of some description; it does not necessarily come from speed alone. Roland Barthes (1972, p.89) observes that there is a homely quality to some cars (he is referring specifically to the Citroen DS19) and notes "a turning from the alchemy of speed to a relish in driving". In part of course this is imposed by speed limits, but it is far more than just a response to these—it is a deep concern with the style and performance of cars, with skill in driving, with the complete experience of machines. It is apparent in magazines like *Drive* of the Automobile Association in Britain, in advertisements for new cars, in the personal ornamentation applied to car interiors and exteriors.

So from the perspective of personal involvement machines serve to create a whole set of involved experiences that mediate between man and landscape. But from other perspectives this mediating role is not so clear.

Machines are used for the outright mastery of environments, making their
own geographies and spaces, averaging land surfaces, shortening distances
and dividing activities. Lefebvre (1971, p.100) comments that "motorized
traffic enables people and objects to congregate and mix without meeting
..., each element remaining enclosed in its own compartment, tucked away
in its own shell". This compartmentalisation is carried into the making of
distinctive environments for machines alone. Highways, parking lots,
filling stations, runways, make no provisions for people not in the
appropriate machine—there is no shelter, no walkway, no humanitarian
gesture (figure 6.11). The result is generally not attractive: "No
landscape", declared Osbert Lancaster (1959, p.186), "was ever enriched
by the addition of a garage, and not even the most besotted modernist can
claim even a functional beauty for the average gas station". Yet this
position has been disputed. J. B. Jackson (1970, p.149), scarcely a
besotted modernist, has suggested of highway strips that their "lighting
effects—not merely the neon signs, but the indirect lighting of filling
stations and drive-ins—are often extremely handsome; so are the bright
clear colours of the buildings and installations". And Robert Venturi
(1972) has written lavishly in praise of the highway strips of Las Vegas.
The arguments of Jackson and Venturi are good from the viewpoint of the
automobile driver; Lancaster's comments are equally good from the
perspective of the poor pedestrian lost in this machine geography. We
cannot have the pleasures and freedoms of machines and the local,
handmade landscapes of the horse and carriage. And however much we
may regret it the horse and carriage is obsolete, the present-day landscapes
we know best are the view *of* the road, in which we are of necessity
closely involved, and the view *from* the road of passing, middle-distance,
often absurd landscapes.

7.5 The everyday landscape
Henri Lefebvre (1971, pp.100–101) suggests that cars direct behaviour in
fields ranging from speech to economics, are substitutes for eroticism, for
adventure, for human contact, and are the leading objects in everyday
life. Everyday life comprises all that is humble, ordinary, and taken for
granted; it is made up of repetitions, of small gestures and insignificant
actions in which all the elements relate to each other in such a regular
sequence or accepted pattern that their meaning need never be questioned;
it includes all those experiences, such as those of landscape through
machines, that are readily and unselfconsciously accepted. The everyday
can be characterised negatively in terms of its separation from the modern,
that which is original or brilliant: great scientific and technical
demonstrations have relevance to the everyday only as distant myths.
It is characterised, too, by a decay of the skill and care that once was
manifest in the production of all things; these are replaced by mass-
produced objects and images that are readily consumed by the public.

In everyday life a sense of social responsibility has been outmoded by a desire for individual freedom and comfort. Everyday life is the life that most of us lead most of the time.

Everyday life has an everyday landscape which can include great and original megastructures, city halls, piazzas, and totally designed settings that are so completely taken for granted that their once exceptional features have been reduced to ordinary and unselfconsciously accepted backgrounds. The everyday landscape is perhaps more easily understood as all the commonplace objects, spaces, ᷓ ᷓdings, and activities that we accept as comprising the setting for daily routines. It has lurid signs, car parks, wires, sidesplits and semidetached houses, corner stores and filling stations. It is often ugly and chaotic, looks awful in many different ways, but it is in some respects a vital mess because it is unpretentious and uncontrived and a more or less unselfconscious expression of peoples' activities and wants. It is, however, promoted and exploited by salesmen, who, while participating themselves in everyday life, endeavour to control and guide consumption, activities, and wants.

Perhaps the two clearest forms of the everyday landscape are highway strips and suburban developments, both of which are made possible by and structured in response to automobiles. They have been criticised respectively for creating confusion and monotony: Robert Venturi (1966, p.59), making a plea for striking a balance in planning and architecture writes: "It seems our fate now to be faced with either the endless inconsistencies of Roadtown, which is chaos, or the infinite consistency of Levittown, which is boredom. In Roadtown we have a false complexity: in Levittown a false simplicity". False complexity and false simplicity may be the two aesthetic poles of everyday landscape, but they are scarcely valid descriptions of our normal experiences of these settings. In fact the strip and the subdivision are declarations of present-day values. "The strip", writes Grady Clay (1973, p.108), "is trying to tell us something about ourselves: namely that most Americans prefer convenience, are determined to simplify as much of the mechanical, service and distribution side of life as possible, and are willing to subsidize any informal, geographic behaviour setting that helps." This applies even more to shopping plazas which combine all the commercialism directed towards everyday life with drive-in convenience, with rational distribution systems, with efficient use of land and even with a pedestrian mall ideal. And suburban housing tracts, uniform and monotonous though they may appear, also declare contemporary values. Experienced as the setting of daily life, a mature suburban street is attractive and tidy because everyone maintains his property; it is reasonably quiet, safe, a good place to try out your gardening skills for neighbours and passers-by to see, a nice place to live (figures 5.6, 6.11).

Yet the everyday landscape is ordinary, lacking in distinction, without high points or surprises. It is largely inauthentic in that it has been designed *for* people and is filled with mass-produced objects. There is no great commitment to their landscape among those living in subdivisions and using commercial strips—these have a shallow exchangeable significance and even the privately-owned house is regarded as little more than an investment. Such shallowness does not matter for most of the time— indeed in the mobile and changeful present-day society a lack of commitment to place and landscape is an advantage, for moves can then be made without regret. The everyday landscape functions well enough, it is reasonably comfortable, and has sense of vitality and honesty that derives from the fact that these are the immediate settings of daily life. And it is largely for this reason that Robert Venturi (1966, p.103) can hopefully suggest that "it is from the everyday landscape, vulgar and disdained, that we can draw the complex and contradictory order that is valid for our architecture as an urbanistic whole".

7.6 Confusion and proteanism in present-day landscapes
A rational landscape, created from the perspective of intentional rationality, can nevertheless be experienced as absurd, as alien and impenetrable, and yet it can also be taken for granted as the setting for everyday life. In short, landscapes change their identity according to the way in which we experience them. Furthermore the very settings themselves often appear to be chaotic and confused—cities seem to have no clear limits, the countryside is industrialised, ribbon developments seem to have a mishmash of land uses, and scenes that only last year were nicely unspoilt have disappeared without trace beneath reservoirs, houses, new airports, or whatever. The result is that our sense of order is challenged, and our images of how landscapes ought to be no longer fit with our experiences. "Our distorted surroundings", suggests Gyorgy Kepes (1956, p.69), "by distorting us have robbed us of the power to make our experiences coherent." We find increasingly that we are confronted and confused by landscapes that lack clear centres and boundaries and which are constantly changing identity.

'Protean man' is the name used by R. J. Lifton (1969) to describe what he believes is a peculiarly modern form of personality or individual identity. Protean man, as the name implies, changes his identity almost at will as he shifts from life-style to life-style, trying out new options and exploring alternatives; middle-class youths become radical students, then conservative businessmen, then concerned activists. There is of course some degree of continuity in personality, but it is the *break* with established patterns and continuing beliefs that is most apparent: each new way of life is adopted in its entirety. Lifton argues that protean man represents a major shift from the traditional view that each individual should present a consistent and stable identity throughout his life; he is part of modern culture in which stability and consistency and the boundaries of things are not clearly defined. For example, nuclear weapons do not distinguish between citizen and soldier, the guilty and the innocent; mass media overwhelm us with indiscriminate images that mix reality and fantasy, enjoyment and blatant commercialism; modern international corporations are monolithic yet formless, they interpenetrate all aspects of our lives, changing their style freely to fit the particular product that is being marketed.

Proteanism and the blurring of boundaries are widely evident in present-day landscapes (figures 6.1, 6.4, 6.11, 6.12). Regions in which local materials and technologies are manifest in distinctive landscapes exist now only as relict features and are usually much modified by the forces of placelessness. Instead of discrete regions with coherent and persisting identities there are landscapes that are without clear centres or edges, undergoing continuous and complex changes. The tallest building in the restless skyline of downtown Toronto has been consecutively overtopped five times in the last ten years; suburbs everywhere have oozed amorphously outwards at rates measurable in miles per year. Fashions in the facades of mass produced houses, in the style of signs, in cars, in thoughts to adopt and theories to apply, are adjusted every year: the progressive public architecture of the 1950s, the airports of the 1960s, the planning principles in favour only a few years ago, the Mediterranean style houses of last year, are dated or obsolete long before they are worn out.

As the rate of these protean changes in landscapes increases, the variations of landscapes from region to region decrease. International styles in architecture of all types, in demands for products and in the products created to satisfy those demands, reduce the differences between places. The retail outlets of multinational corporations have standardised signs, logos, colours, fittings and services (e.g. Crosby, 1973, p.144). These outlets, suggests Stephen Kurtz (1973, p.20), belong to that "class of infinities exemplified by rings and labyrinths, which have no beginning and no end"; the way in and the way out is everywhere. Such uniformities contradict our expectations about the distinctiveness of separate places, and as tourists or migrants we may often find ourselves looking for the familiar rather than the unusual. In some ways this uniformity may make for confusion, but by providing a measure of familiarity from city to city these placeless retail and service chains and architectures may help to make tolerable the high rates of mobility that characterise present-day life. Sameness provides continuity in our experiences of different settings—a continuity that is extremely important because it compensates for the experiential and identity changes we undergo in new environments. Grady Clay (1973, p.110) writes: "The moment we move we acquire other names, and become newcomers, strangers, migrants, tourists, commuters ... . As tourists, paraders or travellers we may shed one self for another and turn into spendthrifts, lechers and litterbugs" (figure 6.2).

Changes in form and fashion, our own mobility, and shifts in experience mean that we frequently confront landscapes we have not learned to recognise or cannot understand. In his study of the Oxfordshire landscape Lionel Brett (1965, p.66) has a photograph of a large plastic thing in a field which he can only describe as "a Really Exciting Thing in a Field". Grady Clay (1973, p.127) uses the word 'stacks' to describe "huge piled-up masses of something or other" that loom quietly as backdrops in thousands of neighbourhoods. These blank confrontations with anonymous objects are surprisingly common—even the familiar shapes of international architecture disguise the nature of the activities within. And this denseness of individual features is exacerbated by patterns that have no obvious explanation—empty lots in city centres where land values are clearly at a premium are used as car parks; new office buildings, such as Centrepoint in central London, remain empty and unused several years after completion, shopping centres are built midway between towns where nobody lives. Speculation, taxation, zoning, least distance locations, may offer reasonable explanations for such anomalies, but the patterns they produce in landscapes are obscure and not easily grasped.

Obscurity, uniformity, and proteanism in landscapes are expressions of new processes and values in society. They are sources of confusion, not merely because they are chaotic in themselves, but also because they break with our inherited and established images of how landscapes should be organised and because we have few contemporary and appropriate images. Gyorgy Kepes (1956, p.18) has written:

"When unprecedented aspects of nature confront us, our world model inherited from the past becomes strained; the new territory does not belong to it. Disoriented, we become confused and shocked. We may even create monsters, using old outworn images and symbols in an inverted negative way. Manipulating them, amplifying them, we invent new Minotaurs and new mazes until we find new meanings and symbols growing from the new world."

For the moment, at least, it seems that we either have to accept the confusions with which modern landscapes present us, or we must block out selectively all those features that we cannot fit into our established images.

7.7 The simple landscape
There is a major paradox in present-day landscapes. On the one hand they appear to be confused and comprised of changing patterns; this is especially so for relationships in and between landscapes. On the other hand present-day landscapes often seem to be simple and superficial, naively obvious; this is the case particularly on a small scale and within specific settings.

The simple landscape is the landscape that declares itself openly, presents no problems or surprises, lacks subtlety; there are none of the ambiguities and contradictions and complexities that Venturi (1966) argues lend meaning to buildings and man-made environments; there are no deep significances, only a turning to the obvious and a separation of different functions into distinct units. It is found particularly where environments have been rationally designed in the systematic hierarchical way described by Christopher Alexander (1966)—for instance, in new towns, military camps, industrial parks, suburban subdivisions and public housing projects. These have a number of characteristics that distinguish them from the complexities of many unselfconsciously designed and evolved landscapes. First, the simple landscape is orderly—things are laid out in a predictable way, behaviour has been anticipated, there are no inconsistencies or surprises (figure 6.15). Second, it is almost always unifunctional: one building–one purpose, one planning zone–one purpose; activities are neatly divided and related to each other by efficient communication systems. The architects and planners of the simple landscape tend to practise what Venturi (1966, p.23) calls the "easy unity of exclusion" rather than the "difficult unity of inclusion". Third, and this is related to unifunction, the simple landscape is univalent—each element in it has its own significance and identity which is not related to any higher unity except through proximity. Fourth, there is a levelling of experiences; there may be possibilities for sensations but these are discrete, ephemeral, and unencumbered by catharsis or other emotional upsets and involvements. And fifth, the simple landscape is of the present; it may possess intimations of the past and the future, but these are bowdlerised to fit with popular and idealised images.

Morse Peckham (1965) has argued that a major function of artistic works of all kinds is to raise doubts and confusions; no purpose could be further from the apparent aims of the simple landscape; indeed it seems as if it has been built to avoid all doubts and questions and to fall wholly within the values of the established order. In the simple landscape, as in advertisements and coffee table books about scenery, there is no conflict or hardship or ugliness or distastefulness.

Ontario Place is a modern fun-palace recreational complex in Toronto funded, designed, and built by the Government of Ontario for reasons that remain obscure (the initiative and drive for its construction apparently came from civil servants rather than politicians). It is an archetypal illustration of simple landscape—a totally fabricated, traffic-free environment situated on several man-made islands in Lake Ontario (figure 6.10). It consists of several activity areas—a "Children's Village", an "18-hole par 44 Alice in Wonderland mini-golf course", an open-air theatre for 2000 people (the Forum), a marina for those who can afford it and paddle boats for those who cannot, a restaurant and boutique area, a geodesic dome (the Cinesphere) for supermovies shown on a "giant screen six stories high", a "famed naval vessel HMCS Haida", a launch pad for helicopter sightseeing rides, and several pods (structures on stilt above the lake) that house multimedia exhibitions in "experiential theatres '. The pods are connected by a system of long corridors that direct visi ɔrs and viewers in one direction only—once started on a selected route it is surprisingly difficult to deviate from it because there are numeroι barred entrances and NO ENTRY signs. Each activity is separated from its neighbouring and unrelated activities by a no-man's land of grass oɪ water.

It is all clean and pleasant, modern and functional, but slightly fɪivolous, vaguely utopian, definitely suburban. All of which is not to suggest that Ontario Place is a failure. It is, on the contrary, very popular for it provides new and undemanding experiences for people from all sectorᵎ of society. It is simple because it possesses an obviousness and a predictab ty, a lack of contradiction and ambiguity. There is nothing sinister or dirty, nothing that you might not want your children to see. Ultimately perhaps there is nothing here that is really interesting or challenging or that will make a lasting impression on visitors. Ontario Place is a nice, straightforward landscape that epitomises all the numerous other simple landscapes of the present-day.

7.8 Significance in the present-day landscape

Symbols, the theologian Paul Tillich (1958) suggested, point to something beyond themselves and open up levels of reality which are otherwise closed; they cannot be produced intentionally but grow and die. The landscapes of nonliterate and traditional cultures were full with symbols in which most members of the culture participated; buildings and landforms and city plans often had sacred meanings and cosmological forms (Tuan, 1974). Such symbols expressed profound meanings in and attachments to landscape, and maintained those meanings and attachments. The present-day landscape is, in contrast, characterised by signs pointing not to deeper levels of reality but to overriding sets of ideas or "myths" that are often contrived and deliberately fabricated. The significances of modern landscapes lie especially in these signs and their associated myths.

A sign, as Roland Barthes explains (1972), is not simply a directional or descriptive message, but part of any system of communication whether language or photography or landscape. It is made up of two terms—the signifier and the signified—which combine perfectly to form the third, the sign itself. For example, the Jacey Cinema in Leicester Square in London has for its exterior decoration the title of the current movie in huge black letters (in May 1975 it was TRUCK STOP WOMEN X) on a lurid pink background, with photos of more or less naked women arranged around the entrance (= the signifier). All of which signifies that risqué movies are shown inside, though the 'X' rating serves to indicate that they are not so pornographic that they fall outside the realm of the censor (= the signified).

The exterior itself, by the scale of the letters, the colours and lewd pictures, is 'eroticised', and strictly speaking in terms of our experience there is only this eroticised facade (= the sign). But this facade is merely the first term in another system of signs, for by its very presence in the centre of London it signifies permissiveness, that we live in a tolerant, liberal society. This is a popular myth supported by books, magazines, and all the media. Of course, when we see the Jacey Cinema, or any of its innumerable counterparts around the world, we are not aware of all these analytic phases; our impression is simply of the eroticised cinema and some of the possibilities it suggests. And even if this impression and these possibilities are brought into question, for instance by the sight of the vagrants in Leicester Square, it does not deny the myth, for as Barthes (1972, p.130) argues it is the first impact of a myth that is most important —"A more attentive reading of the myth in no way increases its power or its ineffectiveness: a myth is at the same time imperfectible and unquestionable; time or knowledge will not make it better or worse."

The landscapes of present-day society express the myths of reason, of the ideal past and the ideal future, of progress and permissiveness, of individual freedom and material comfort, of Swissness for winter and Mediterraneity for summer, and logs for North-American pioneers. Barthes (1972, pp.124–125) clarifies the role of such myths by reference to Basque architecture: in the Basque region of Spain he may identify a common style of building, but he does not feel concerned by it—"I see only too well that it was here before me, without me". But on seeing in suburban Paris a "natty white chalet with red tiles and dark-brown half timbering ... I feel as if I were receiving an imperious injunction to name this object a Basque chalet: or even better, to see it as the very essence of Basquity". It stands out, calling attention to itself as Basque, even though details of design have been changed and the distinctive features have been applied to an anonymous shell and the building has no history. It is superficially Basque, frozen in space and time. And, of course, not just single buildings but whole areas and landscapes can be given such mythical identities; thus entire subdivisions of mock Tudor houses in North-American cities capitalise on the dual myths of Englishness and ideal history. But it is not always necessary for the settings themselves to be made in the image of a preexisting myth, for, as Grady Clay (1973, p.61) suggests, a little skilful fabulation and salesmanship can serve to convert any local identity into a money-making proposition: Atlanta capitalises on its Gone-with-the-Wind image, Stratford-on-Avon has Shakespeare, and in the travel guide *Explore Canada* we read of Fort Steele in British Columbia: "An East Kootenay town of the 1890–1905 period was created here in the 1960s". People apparently do see what they believe and what they have been persuaded to believe.

The major feature of these myths that infuse present-day landscapes is their simplicity. Barthes writes (1972, p.143): "Myth gives human acts the simplicity of essences, does away with all dialectics, with any going back beyond what is immediately visible, it organises a world that is without contradictions because it is without depth, a world wide open and wallowing in the evident, it establishes a blissful clarity; things appear to mean something by themselves". Myths also offer innoculation against that which is undesirable or unattractive, either by introducing what is distasteful in elements large enough to be noticed but too small to be upsetting, or by simply embracing them as problems to be resolved. Myth lacks history: "Nothing is produced, nothing is chosen: all one has to do is to possess these new objects from which all soiling trace of origin or choice has been removed" (Barthes, 1972, p.151). Myths reduce all otherness to sameness—nothing is really different, except of course when something is so different it cannot be assimilated and then it is 'exotic'. And myths reduce quality to quantity, everything is reasoned and measured, if not by numbers then by precise effects.

These are the principal features of the myths that embrace present-day landscapes; they constitute the foundation for social agreement about the qualities of those landscapes as well as the means for control of experience and consumption through advertising and the other means of making and maintaining myths. The cultural meaning of present-day landscapes goes little further than the significances of myths that provide the basis for the creation of these landscapes and the context for our experiences of them.

7.9 Concluding comments

The difficulties which we have in coping with the present-day landscape have been particularly well summarised by Gyorgy Kepes (1965, p.i). He writes: "Expelled from the smaller friendlier world in which previous centuries of men moved with a confidence born of familiarity, we are today compelled to cope with an expanded scale of events in a big alien redefined world ... . We have not yet found our places in this redefined world". Places with settings which are not only distinctively local and reflect a continuity of style and tradition, but also constitute profound centres of care and existence, are indeed part of an old cultural order; and although we may look back to them nostalgically they have no active part to play in the new landscape. The new landscape is characterised not by its profound meanings and its symbols, but by rationality and absurdity and its separation from us. It is characterised too by its everydayness as the ordinary and unexceptional background to our daily lives, by its confusion that results from a lack of focuses, discrete regions, or any familiar pattern, and by its simplicity and obviousness.

Placelessness is not merely in context in these present-day landscapes— it is an essential part of them and a product of them. Rationalism and absurdity undermine commitment to place, everydayness and simplicity promote uniformity, proteanism destroys existing places. The roots of significance in the present-day landscape are shallow indeed; there is little scope for the development of more than a casual sense of place because the identities of places are merely the product of fabulations or of local associations of universal and placeless processes.

These descriptions of the landscapes we live in may appear to be largely negative, but this is a misleading conclusion to draw because it is based on criteria that relate to the old images of stability and clearly-defined and cared-for places. We do not assess modern political economy in terms appropriate to medieval society—that clearly would be foolish; but most of the terms that we have for describing landscapes seem to be those suited to the idealised handicraft landscapes of some earlier period, and it is inevitable that when these are applied to the present they should seem pejorative. Obviously our experiences of present-day landscapes are not all worthless and distasteful, we do not spend all our moments of attention to landscape in moods of grim cynicism and resignation. There is much in our contemporary environments that is pleasant and attractive, many buildings and developments are dramatic and exciting; and while our experiences may have a shallowness they also have great breadth, placelessness also means freedom from place, and everydayness means comfort and security as well as entrapment in a bureaucratic consumer society.

The present-day landscape has, in short, a generally comfortable and quite efficient geography, even though it lacks depth and variety and tends to eradicate past geographies. It is a landscape quite in accord with the dominant attitudes in present-day society. But whether we judge this landscape to be an ugly mess or to be the manifestation of a new age of prosperity, progress, and equality, one thing about it is apparent. It is a recent phenomenon and there is no reason to believe that its features will last for ever, that convenience and efficiency must necessarily involve absurdity and placelessness, or that there are no prospects for profoundly significant places within this present-day landscape.

Prospects for places

There are at least two experienced geographies: there is a geography of places, characterised by variety and meaning, and there is a placeless geography, a labyrinth of endless similarities. The current scale of the destruction and replacement of the distinctive places of the world suggests that placeless geography is increasingly the more forceful of these, even though a considerable diversity of places persists. It is not immediately apparent whether this persistence is the remnant of an old place-making tradition and is shortly to disappear beneath a tide of uniformity, or whether there exist ongoing and developing sources of diversity that can be encouraged. In other words the prospects for a geography of places are uncertain, but one possibility is the inevitable spread of placelessness, and an alternative possibility is the transcending of placelessness through the formulation and application of an approach for the design of a lived-world of significant places. In this concluding chapter these possibilities are considered in the context of summaries of the main features of place and placelessness.

8.1 Place

Places are fusions of human and natural order and are the significant centres of our immediate experiences of the world. They are defined less by unique locations, landscape, and communities than by the focusing of experiences and intentions onto particular settings. Places are not abstractions or concepts, but are directly experienced phenomena of the lived-world and hence are full with meanings, with real objects, and with ongoing activities. They are important sources of individual and communal identity, and are often profound centres of human existence to which people have deep emotional and psychological ties. Indeed our relationships with places are just as necessary, varied, and sometimes perhaps just as unpleasant, as our relationships with other people.

Experience of place can range in scale from part of a room to an entire continent, but at all scales places are whole entities, syntheses of natural and man-made objects, activities and functions, and meanings given by intentions. Out of these components the identity of a particular place is moulded, but they do not define this identity—it is the special quality of insideness and the experience of being inside that sets places apart in space. Insideness may relate to and be reflected in a physical form, such as the walls of a medieval town, or it may be expressed in rituals and repeated activities that maintain the peculiar properties of a place. But above all it is related to the intensity of experience of a place. Alan Gussow (1971?, p.27) has written of this: "The catalyst that converts any physical location—any environment if you will—into a place, is the process of experiencing deeply. A place is a piece of the whole environment that has been claimed by feelings."

It is possible to distinguish several levels of experience of the insideness of places, and it is perhaps these that tell us most about the nature of the phenomenon of place. At the deepest levels there is an unselfconscious, perhaps even subconscious, association with place. It is home, where your roots are, a centre of safety and security, a field of care and concern, a point of orientation. Such insideness is individual but also intersubjective, a personal experience with which many people can sympathise; it is the essence of a sense of place. And it is perhaps presymbolic and universal insofar as it is an aspect of profound place experience anywhere, yet is not associated with the culturally defined meanings of specific places. This is, in fact, existential insideness—the unselfconscious and authentic experience of place as central to existence. The next level of experience is also authentic and unselfconscious, but it is cultural and communal rather than individual: it involves a deep and unreflective participation in the symbols of a place for what they are. It is associated particularly with the sacred experience of involvement in holy places, and with the secular experience of being known in and knowing the named and significant places of a home region. At a shallower level of insideness there is an authentic sense of place that is selfconscious, and which involves a deliberate attempt to appreciate fully the significance of places without the adoption of narrow intellectual or social conventions and fashions. This is the experience of a sensitive and open-minded outsider seeking to grasp places for what they are to those who dwell in them and for what they mean to him. It is an attitude of particular importance in terms of the possibilities it offers to contemporary and authentic place-making. In contrast is the superficial level of insideness, which involves simply being in a place without attending in any sensitive way to its qualities or significances. Though each of us must experience many of the places we visit like this, since concern with our activities takes precedence and it becomes impossible to concentrate on the place itself, when this is the only form of experience of place it denotes a real failure to 'see' or to be involved in places. For those swayed by the easy charms of mass culture or the cool attractions of technique this does seem to be the primary, perhaps the only, way of experiencing environments; and consequently they feel no care or commitment for places: they are geographically alienated.

The various levels of insideness are manifest in the creation of distinctive types of places. The deep levels of existential insideness are apparent in the unselfconscious making of places which are human in their scale and organisation, which fit both their physical and cultural contexts and hence are as varied as those contexts, and which are filled with significances for those who live in them. Authentic and selfconscious insideness offers a similar, though less completely involved, possibility for expressing man's humanity in places. In both instances "the making of places is", as

Rapoport (1972, p.3-3-10) writes, "the ordering of the world", for it differentiates the world into qualitatively distinct centres and gives a structure that both reflects and guides experiences. This is not so with incidental insideness, for such non-commitment opens the way for the development of environments ordered by conceptual principles or mass fashions rather than by patterns of direct experience. In short, uncommitted insideness is the basis for placelessness.

8.2 Placelessness

Placelessness describes both an environment without significant places and the underlying attitude which does not acknowledge significance in places. It reaches back into the deepest levels of place, cutting roots, eroding symbols, replacing diversity with uniformity and experiential order with conceptual order. At its most profound it consists of a pervasive and perhaps irreversible alienation from places as the homes of men: "He who has no home now will not build one anymore", Rilke declared, and this was echoed by Heidegger—"Homelessness is becoming a world fate" (both cited in Pappenheim, 1959, p.33). At less deep levels placelessness is the adoption of the attitude described by Harvey Cox (1968, p.424) as an "abstract geometric view of place, denuded of its human meaning", and it is manifest in landscapes that can be aptly described by Stephen Kurtz' specific account (1973, p.23) of Howard Johnson's restaurants: "Nothing calls attention to itself; it is all remarkably unremarkable ... . You have seen it, heard it, experienced it all before, and yet ... you have seen and experienced nothing ..."

As a selfconsciously adopted posture placelessness is particularly apparent in *technique*, the overriding concern with efficiency as an end in itself. In *technique* places can be treated as the interchangeable, replaceable locations of things, as indeed they are by multinational corporations, powerful central governments, and uninvolved planners. As an unselfconscious attitude placelessness is particularly associated with mass culture—the adoption of fashions and ideas about landscapes and places that are coined by a few 'experts' and disseminated to the people through the mass media. The products of these two attitudes are combined in uniform, sterile, other-directed, and kitschy places—places which have few significances and symbols, only more or less gaudy signs and things performing functions with greater or lesser efficiency. The overall result is the undermining of the importance of place for both individuals and cultures, and the casual replacement of the diverse and significant places of the world with anonymous spaces and exchangeable environments.

8.3 The inevitability of placelessness?

"The places that we have known belong now only to the little world of
space on which we map them for our own convenience. None of them
was ever more than a thin slice held between the contiguous
impressions that composed our life at that time; remembrance for a
particular form is but regret for a particular moment, and houses, roads,
avenues, are as fugitive, alas, as the years."

Thus Marcel Proust (1970, p.288) expressed with nostalgia the insignificance
of places for modern man. No more is there the "sense of continuity with
place" which Harvey Cox (1968, p.423) believes is so necessary for
people's sense of reality and so essential for their identity; the meanings
of places have become as ephemeral as their physical forms. Cox judges
this as "one of the most deplorable characteristics of our time", but
deplore it, condemn it, criticise it as we might, there often appears to be
little that can be done to prevent the diminishing of significant relations
with places.

The prospect of inevitable placelessness is supported by Jacques Ellul's
view of *technique*, one of the main forces behind the developing placeless
geography. He writes (1964, p.436): "The attitude of scientists, at any
rate, is clear. Technique exists because it is technique. The golden age
will be because it will be. Any other answer is superfluous." In other
words *technique* has a drive of its own that is universal, we can no longer
think in terms other than those of *technique* because it is the only
language we know, and the only possibility is that placelessness will come
to dominate. If we regret the disappearance of significant places this is
only sentimentality and we should at least acknowledge the benefits of the
new geography. As George Grant (1969, p.138) expresses it: "It might
be said that the older systems of meaning have been replaced by a new
one. The enchantment of our souls by myth, philosophy or revelation
has been replaced by a more immediate meaning—the building of free and
equal men by the overcoming of chance." But in what sense freedom and
in what sense equality? To master chance in human and non-human nature
requires the most efficient use of *technique* that is possible, and that in
turn requires the perfection of science and powerful central government.
Louch (1966, p.239) has declared: "Totalitarianism is too weak a word
and too inefficient an instrument to describe the perfect scientific
society." Alexis de Tocqueville (1945, vol.II, p.337) wrote: "The will
of man is not shattered but softened, bent and guided—such centralised
power does not destroy, but compresses, enervates, extinguishes and
stupefies a people."

If Tocqueville, Grant, and Ellul are correct, and in the landscape of
industrial cultures there is massive evidence to support them, then
opposition to *technique* and to central authorities—two of the primary
sources of placelessness—seems either futile or impossible. We may

protest it, deplore it, propose alternatives to it, but the fundamental basis for our experience of the landscapes we live in is increasingly becoming the attitude of placelessness.

8.4 Designing a lived-world of places

But such pessimism and fatalism are not yet justified. There may indeed come a time when placelessness is inevitable because it is the only geography we know, but so long as there are what Grant (1969, p.139) calls "intimations of authentic deprival", then the possibility of some different way of thinking and acting must remain. David Brower (in Gussow, 1971?, p.15) is in fact quite specific about what must be done: "The best weapon against the unending deprivation that would be the consequence of ... unending demand is a revival of man's sense of place." How this is to be achieved he does not make clear, but it is certain that loss of attachment to places and the decline of the ability to make places authentically do constitute real deprivations, and that the redevelopment of such attachments and abilities is essential if we are to create environments that do not have to be ignored or endured. Furthermore, there appears to be a possibility of doing this outside the context of *technique*, for sense of place is in its essence both prescientific and intersubjective.

The possibilities for maintaining and reviving man's sense of place do not lie in the preservation of old places—that would be museumisation; nor can they lie in a selfconscious return to the traditional ways of place-making—that would require the regaining of a lost state of innocence. Instead, placelessness must be transcended. "That human activity should become more dispersed is inevitable", Georges Matoré (1966, p.6) has written, "but to compensate let the occupied, lived-in space acquire more cohesion, become as rich as possible, and grow large with the experience of living." Similarly Harvey Cox (1968, p.424) has argued that beyond the stage of homogeneous space, in which every place is interchangeable with every other place, lies a stage of human space in which "space is for man and places are understood as giving pace, variety and orientation to man". This will not come about automatically but through deliberate effort and the development of 'secularisation', an attitude which corresponds closely to selfconscious authenticity. Secularisation "dislodges ancient oppressions and overturns stultifying conventions. It turns man's social and cultural life over to him, demanding a constant expenditure of vision and competence" (Cox, 1965, p.86). While the danger always remains of this being short-circuited by new orthodoxies that will result in placelessness, secularisation provides a very real basis for optimism about places so long as we can live up to the responsibilities it demands. Cox continues: "A secular civilisation need not be monochrome or homogeneous. But the character lent by diversity cannot be left to chance. Like everything else in the secular city variety must be planned or it does not happen."

The creating of a variety of places which give pace, orientation, and identity to man is clearly no simple task. It involves what Nairn (1965, p.93) has called "the terrific assumption" that "each place is different, that each case must be decided on its own merits, that completely different solutions may be needed for apparently similar cases". To acknowledge this does not mean that humanist place-making must be chaotic and unstructured, but rather that its order must be derived from significant experience and not from arbitrary abstractions and concepts as represented on maps and plans. The implication is that selfconscious and authentic place-making is not something that can be done programmatically. A method like that developed by Christopher Alexander (Alexander, 1964, 1966; Alexander and Poyner, 1970), based on the decomposition of sets of environmental objects and activities into their atomic elements, and the reconstitution of these into a design solution, does have considerable value for improving current design strategies and possibly for achieving designs that fit local situations well; and approaches like Gordon Cullen's analysis (1971) of the structures of visual experience of townscape are potentially of great use in improving the quality of appearance of landscapes. But these, and almost all the other procedures of environmental design, are either too formal and too rigidly prescriptive, or they treat experience and meaning only as other variables capable of manipulation.

What is needed is not a precisely mathematical procedure that treats the environments we live in like some great machine that we do not yet quite understand, but an approach to the design of the lived-world of both everyday and exceptional experiences—an approach that is wholly selfconscious yet does seek to create wholly designed environments into which people must be fitted, an approach that is responsive to local structures of meaning and experience, to particular situations and to the variety of levels of meaning of place; an approach that takes its inspiration from the existential significance of place, the need that many people have for a profound attachment to places, and the ontological principles of dwelling and sparing identified by Heidegger (Vycinas, 1961). Such an approach cannot provide precise solutions to clearly defined problems, but, proceeding from an appreciation of the significance of place and the particular activities and local situations, it would perhaps provide a way of outlining some of the main directions and possibilities, thus allowing scope for individuals and groups to make their own places, and to give those places authenticity and significance by modifying them and by dwelling in them.

David Brower (in Gussow, 1971?, p.15) has written that "the places we have roots in, and the flavour of their light and sound and feel when things are right in those places, are the wellsprings of our serenity". It is not possible to design rootedness nor to guarantee that things will be right in places, but it is perhaps possible to provide conditions that will allow roots and care for places to develop. To do this is no easy task, and indeed how or whether such a complex synthesis of procedure and sentiment can be achieved in designing a lived-world of places is by no means clear. But if places matter to us, if we are at all concerned about the psychological consequences and moral issues in uprooting and increasing geographical mobility and placelessness, then we must explore the possibility of developing an approach for making places selfconsciously and authentically. The only alternatives are to celebrate and participate in the glorious non-place urban society, or to accept in silence the trivialisation and careless eradication of the significant places of our lives. And, as Sinclair Gauldie (1969, p.182) has written: "To live in an environment which has to be endured or ignored rather than enjoyed is to be diminished as a human being."

8.5 Conclusion

A deep human need exists for associations with significant places. If we choose to ignore that need, and to allow the forces of placelessness to continue unchallenged, then the future can only hold an environment in which places simply do not matter. If, on the other hand, we choose to respond to that need and to transcend placelessness, then the potential exists for the development of an environment in which places are for man, reflecting and enhancing the variety of human experience. Which of these two possibilities is most probable, or whether there are other possibilities, is far from certain. But one thing at least is clear—whether the world we live in has a placeless geography or a geography of significant places, the responsibility for it is ours alone.

References

Abler R, Adams J S, Gould P R, 1971 *Spatial Organisation: The Geographer's View of the World* (Englewood Cliffs, N J: Prentice-Hall)
Alexander C, 1964 *Notes on the Synthesis of Form* (Cambridge, Mass: Harvard University Press)
Alexander C, 1966 "A city is not a tree" *Design* No. 206 47-55
Alexander C, Poyner B, 1970? "The atoms of environmental structure" Working Paper No. 42 Centre for Planning and Development Research, University of California, Berkeley
Allsopp B, 1970 *The Study of Architectural History* (London: Studio Vista)
Arnheim R, 1969 *Visual Thinking* (Berkeley: University of California Press)
Ashby W R, 1965 *Design for a Brain* (London: Chapman and Hall)
Bachelard G, 1969 *The Poetics of Space* (Boston: Beacon Press)
Banham R, 1973 *Los Angeles: The Architecture of Four Ecologies* (Harmondsworth: Penguin)
Bartels D, 1973 "Between theory and metatheory" in *Directions in Geography* Ed R J Chorley (London: Methuen)
Barthes R, 1972 *Mythologies* (London: Jonathan Cape)
Benevolo L, 1967 *The Origins of Modern Town Planning* (Cambridge, Mass: MIT Press)
Berg J H van der, 1965 "The subject and his landscape" in *The Age of Complexity* Ed H Kohl (New York: Mentor Books)
Berger P L, 1971 *A Rumour of Angels* (Harmondsworth: Pelican Books)
Berger P L, Luckmann T, 1967 *The Social Construction of Reality* (Garden City, N Y: Doubleday)
Berger P L, Berger B, Kellner H, 1973 *The Homeless Mind* (New York: Random House)
Berndt R M, Berndt C H, 1970 *Man, Land and Myth in North Australia* (East Lansing: Michigan State University Press)
"Biblelands ...", 1972 "Biblelands project to be developed in Southeast Ohio" *New York Times* Sunday December 17 1972, Section 1, p 27
Blake P, 1964 *God's Own Junkyard* (New York: Holt, Rinehart and Winston)
Blythe R, 1969 *Akenfield* (Harmondsworth: Penguin Books)
Bollnow O, 1967 "Lived space" in *Readings in Existential Phenomenology* Eds N Lawrence, D O'Connor (Englewood Cliffs, N J: Prentice-Hall)
Boulding K, 1961 *The Image* (Ann Arbor: University of Michigan Press)
Brett L, 1965 *Landscape in Distress* (London: The Architectural Press)
Brett L, 1970 *Parameters and Images* (London: Weidenfeld and Nicolson)
Briggs A, 1968 "A sense of place" in *The Fitness of Man's Environment* Smithsonian Annual II (New York: Harper and Row)
Buber M, 1958 *I and Thou* (New York: Charles Scribner's Sons)
Bunge W, 1962 *Theoretical Geography* Lund Studies in Geography, Series C, No. 1, Department of Geography, Royal University of Lund, Sweden
Burton R, 1932 *Anatomy of Melancholy* (London: Dent)
Camus A, 1955 *The Myth of Sisyphus* (New York: Vintage Books)
Camus A, 1959 *Noces suivi de l'Été* (Paris: Editions Gallimard)
Cassirer E, 1970 *An Essay on Man* (Toronto: Bantam Books)
Chardin T de, 1955 *The Phenomenon of Man* (London: Collins)
Choay F, 1969 "Urbanism and semiology" in *Meaning in Architecture* Eds C Jencks, G Baird (London: The Cresset Press)
Chomsky N, 1969 *American Power and the New Mandarins* (New York: Pantheon Books)
Clark K, 1969 *Civilisation* (London: British Broadcasting Corporation)

Clay G, 1973 *Close-Up: How to Read the American City* (London: Pall Mall)
Cobb E, 1970 "The ecology of imagination in childhood" in *The Subversive Science* Eds P Shepard, D McKinley (Boston: Houghton Mifflin)
Coles R, 1970 *Uprooted Children* (New York: Harper and Row)
Coles R, 1972 *Migrants, Sharecroppers, Mountaineers* (Boston: Little Brown)
Coles R, Erikson J, 1971 *The Middle Americans* (Boston: Little Brown)
Cox H, 1965 *The Secular City* (Toronto: Macmillan)
Cox H, 1968 "The restoration of a sense of place" *Ekistics* 25 422-424
Crosby T, 1973 *How to Play the Environment Game* (Harmondsworth: Penguin)
Cross M, (Ed) 1970 *The Frontier Thesis and the Canadas* (Toronto: Copp Clark)
Cullen G, 1971 *The Concise Townscape* (London: The Architectural Press)
Dardel E, 1952 *L'Homme et La Terre: Nature de Realité Géographique* (Paris: Presses Universitaires de France)
Donat J, (Ed) 1967 *World Architecture 4* (London: Studio Vista)
Doob L, 1964 *Patriotism and Nationalism* (New Haven: Yale University Press)
Dubos R, 1972 *A God Within* (New York: Charles Scribner's Sons)
Durrell L, 1969 *The Spirit of Place* (New York: Dutton)
Eckbo G, 1969 "The landscape of tourism" *Landscape* 18 (2) 29-31
Eliade M, 1959 *The Sacred and the Profane* (New York: Harcourt, Brace and World)
Eliade M, 1961 *Images and Symbols* (London: Harrill Press)
Ellul J, 1967 *The Technological Society* (New York: Random House)
Erikson E, 1959 "Identity and the life-cycle" *Psychological Issues* 1 (1)
Ewald W R, (Ed) 1967 *Environment and Man* (Bloomington: Indiana University Press)
Explore Canada, 1974 (Montreal: Reader's Digest-Canadian Automobile Association)
Eyck A van, 1969 "A miracle of moderation" in *Meaning in Architecture* Eds C Jencks G Baird (London: The Cresset Press)
Ferritti F, 1973 "A few words on Disney World: bad adjectives, good verb-enjoy" *New York Times* Sunday February 11 1973, Section 10, pp 4 and 19
Fitzgerald F, 1974 "Vietnam: Reconciliation" *Atlantic Monthly* June pp 16-27
Fowler W W, 1971 *The Religious Experience of the Roman People* (New York: Cooper Square Publishers)
Fried M, 1963 "Grieving for a lost home" in *The Urban Condition* Ed L J Duhl (New York: Basic Books)
Galbraith J K, 1967 *The New Industrial State* (Toronto: New American Library of Canada)
Gauldie S, 1969 *Architecture: The Appreciation of the Arts* I (London: Oxford University Press)
Giedion S, 1963 *Space, Time and Architecture* (Cambridge, Mass: Harvard University Press)
Goodman R, 1971 *After the Planners* (New York: Simon and Schuster)
Grant G, 1969 *Technology and Empire* (Toronto: Anansi)
Greer G G, 1974 "Super colossal amusement parks: America's 15 best" *Better Homes and Gardens* August pp 95-100
Grene M, 1965 *Approaches to a Philosophical Biology* (New York: Basic Books)
Grigson G, 1972 "The writer and his territory" in a Sense of Place *The Times (London) Literary Supplement* July 28
Gropius W, 1943 *Scope of Total Architecture* (New York: Harper and Row)
Gurvitch G, 1971 *The Social Frameworks of Knowledge* (Oxford: Blackwell)
Gussow A, 1971? *A Sense of Place* (San Francisco: Friends of the Earth)
Haag E van den, 1962 "Of happiness and despair we have no measure" in *Man Alone* Eds E Josephson, M Josephson (New York: Dell)
Hallowell I, 1955 *Culture and Experience* (Philadelphia: University of Pennsylvania Press)

Hampton W, 1970 *Community and Democracy* (London: Oxford University Press)
Handlin O, 1951 *The Uprooted* (Boston: Little Brown)
Hartshorne R, 1959 *Perspectives on the Nature of Geography* (Chicago: Rand McNally)
Hawkes J, 1951 *A Land* (London: The Cresset Press)
Hawkins D, 1964 *The Language of Nature* (Garden City, N Y: Doubleday)
Heidegger M, 1958 "An ontological consideration of place" in *The Question of Being* (New York: Twayne Publishers)
Heidegger M, 1962 *Being and Time* (New York: Harper and Row)
Heidegger M, 1969 *Identity and Difference* (New York: Harper and Row)
Heidegger M, 1971 *Poetry, Language, Thought* (New York: Harper and Row)
Henderson G, 1968 *Chartres* (Harmondsworth: Penguin Books)
Hoggart R, 1959 *The Uses of Literacy* (London: Chatto and Windus)
Husserl E, 1958 *Ideas* (London: George Allen and Unwin)
Hutchison B, 1943 *The Unknown Country: Canada and Her People* (Toronto: McClelland and Stewart)
Innis H, 1951 *The Bias of Communication* (Toronto: University of Toronto Press)
Jackson J B, 1970 "Other-directed architecture" in *Landscapes: Selected Writings of J B Jackson* Ed E H Zube (no place of publication given: University of Massachusetts Press)
Jackson J N, 1973 *The Canadian City* (Toronto: McGraw-Hill Ryerson)
James H, 1968 *The American Scene* (London: Rupert-Hart Davis)
James P, 1954 "Introduction" in *American Geography: Inventory and Prospect* Eds P E James, C F Jones (Syracuse, N Y: Syracuse University Press)
James W, 1899 "On a certain blindness in human beings" in *Talks to Teachers on Psychology* (London: Longmans, Green)
Jammer M, 1969 *Concepts of Space* (Cambridge, Mass: Harvard University Press)
Jencks C, 1971 *Architecture 2000: Predictions and Methods* (New York: Praeger)
Jencks C, 1973 *Modern Movements in Architecture* (Garden City, N Y: Doubleday)
Kepes G, 1956 *The New Landscape in Art and Science* (Chicago: Paul Theobald)
Kepes G, (Ed) 1965 *Structure in Art and Science* (New York: George Braziller)
Kierkegaard S, 1962 *The Present Age* (New York: Harper and Row)
Klapp O E, 1969 *Collective Search for Identity* (New York: Holt, Rinehart and Winston)
Kockelmans J J, 1966 *Phenomenology and Physical Science* (Pittsburgh: Duquesne University Press)
Kurtz S, 1973 *Wasteland: Building the American Dream* (New York: Praeger)
Lancaster O, 1959 *Here, of All Places* (London: John Murray)
Langer S, 1953 *Feeling and Form* (New York: Charles Scribner's Sons)
Lawrence D H, 1964 *Studies in Classic American Literature* (London: Heinemann)
Lefebvre H, 1971 *Everyday Life in the Modern World* (New York: Harper and Row)
Lévi-Strauss C, 1967 *Structural Anthropology* (Garden City, N Y: Doubleday)
Lévi-Strauss C, 1971 *Tristes Tropiques* (New York: Atheneum)
Libby S, 1975 "Visiting the iron age in Denmark" *The Toronto Star* January 11 p G1
Lifton R J, 1967 *Death in Life: Survivors of Hiroshima* (New York: Random House)
Lifton R, 1969 *Boundaries* (Toronto: CBC Publications)
Louch A R, 1966 *Explanation and Human Action* (Berkeley: University of California Press)
Lowenthal D, 1961 "Geography, experience and imagination: Towards a geographical epistemology" *Annals* (Association of American Geographers) 51 241-260
Lowenthal D, 1968 "The American scene" *Geographical Review* 58 (1) 61-88
Lowenthal D, 1970 "Recreation habits and values" in *Challenge for Survival* Ed P Dansereau (New York: Columbia University Press)

Lowenthal D, 1975 "Past time, present place: Landscape and memory" *Geographical Review* **65** (1) 1-36

Luijpen W A, 1966 *Phenomenology and Humanism* (Pittsburgh: Duquesne University Press)

Lukermann F, 1961 "The concept of location in classical geography" *Annals* (Association of American Geographers) **51** 194-210

Lukermann F, 1964 "Geography as a formal intellectual discipline and the way in which it contributes to human knowledge" *Canadian Geographer* **8** (4) 167-172

Lynch K, 1960 *The Image of the City* (Cambridge, Mass: MIT Press)

Lynch K, 1972 *What Time Is This Place?* (Cambridge, Mass: MIT Press)

Lyndon D et al, 1962 "Towards making places" *Landscape* **12** (3) 31-41

Maki F, Ohtaka M, 1965 "Some thoughts on collective form" in *Structure Art and Science* Ed G Kepes (New York: George Braziller)

Malinowski B, 1935 *Coral Gardens and Their Magic* Volume 1 (London: George Allen and Unwin)

Mann T, n.d. *The Magic Mountain* (New York: Random House)

Marinetti F T, 1972 *Selected Writings* Eds R W Flint, A A Copotelli (New York: Farrar, Straus and Giroux)

Maslow A H, 1968 *Towards a Psychology of Being* (New York: Van Nostrand Reinhold)

Matoré G, 1962 *L'Espace Humain* (Paris: La Columbe)

Matoré G, 1966 "Existential space" *Landscape* **15** (3) 5-6

May J A, 1970 *Kant's Concept of Geography* University of Toronto, Department of Geography, Research Publication No. 4

McCann W H, 1941 "Nostalgia: A review of the literature" *Psychological Bulletin* **38** 165-182

McCluhan M H, 1964 *Understanding Media* (Toronto: New American Library of Canada)

Merleau-Ponty M, 1962 *The Phenomenology of Perception* (London: Routledge and Kegan Paul)

Merleau-Ponty M, 1967 *The Structure of Behaviour* (Boston: Beacon Press)

Miller H, 1947 *Remember to Remember* (Norfolk, Conn: New Direction Books)

Mills C W, 1956 *The Power Elite* (New York: Oxford University Press)

Minar D W, Greer S, (Eds) 1969 *The Concept of Community* (Chicago: Aldine)

Minkowski E, 1970 *Lived-Time* (Evanston: Northwestern University Press)

Mishan E J, 1967 *The Costs of Economic Growth* (London: Staples Press)

Moles A, 1971 *Le Kitsch* (Paris: Maison Mame)

Morrill R L, 1970 *The Spatial Organisation of Society* (Belmont, California: Wadsworth)

Mumford L, 1961 *The City in History* (New York: Harcourt, Brace and World)

Museum of Fine Arts, Boston, 1970 *Andrew Wyeth* (Boston: Museum of Fine Arts)

Nairn I, 1965 *The American Landscape* (New York: Random House)

Nash R, 1967 *Wilderness and the American Mind* (New Haven: Yale University Press)

National Academy of Science, 1965 *The Science of Geography* Report of the Ad Hoc Committee on Geography, National Academy of Science-National Research Council, Washington

Newcomb R, 1972 "The nostalgia index of historical landscapes of Denmark" in *International Geography,* Transactions of the International Geographical Union, Montreal **1** 441-443

New York Times, 1967 "Man and his world at Expo 67 Montreal" *Section 11 New York Times* April

Nietzsche F, 1955 *Beyond Good and Evil* (Chicago: Henry Regnery)

Norberg-Schulz C, 1965 *Intentions in Architecture* (Cambridge, Mass: MIT Press)

Norberg-Schulz C, 1969 "Meaning in architecture" in *Meaning in Architecture*
    Ed C Jencks (London: The Cresset Press)
Norberg-Schulz C, 1971 *Existence, Space and Architecture* (New York: Praeger)
Oakeshott M, 1962 *Rationalism in Politics* (London: Methuen)
Olson R G, 1962 *An Introduction to Existentialism* (New York: Dover)
Paassen C van, 1957 *The Classical Tradition of Geography* (Groningen: J B Wolters)
Pappenheim F, 1959 *The Alienation of Modern Man* (New York: Modern Reader
    Paperbacks)
Passmore J, 1968 *A Hundred Years of Philosophy* (Harmondsworth: Pelican Books)
Patton C P, Alexander C S, Kramer F L, 1970 *Physical Geography* (Belmont, California:
    Wadsworth)
Pawley M, 1971 *Architecture Versus Housing* (New York: Praeger)
Peckham M, 1965 *Man's Rage for Chaos* (Philadelphia: Chilton Books)
Piaget J, 1968 *Six Psychological Essays* (Ed D Elkind) (New York: Vintage Books)
Piaget J, 1971 *The Construction of Reality in the Child* (New York: Ballantine Books)
Portmann A, 1959 "The seeing eye" *Landscape* 9 14-21
Prince H, 1961 "The geographical imagination" *Landscape* 11 22-25
Proust M, 1970 *Swann's Way*, Part Two (London: Chatto and Windus)
Raglan Lord, 1964 *The Temple and the House* (London: Routledge and Kegan Paul)
Rapoport A, 1969 *House Form and Culture* (Englewood Cliffs, N J: Prentice-Hall)
Rapoport A, 1972 "Australian aborigines and the definition of place" *Environmental
    Design: Research and Practice* Ed W J Mitchell, Volume 1, Proceedings of the 3rd
    EDRA Conference, Los Angeles, pp 3-3-1 to 3-3-14
Rasmussen S E, 1964 *Experiencing Architecture* (Cambridge, Mass: MIT Press)
Rudofsky B, 1964 *Architecture without Architects* (Garden City, N Y: Doubleday)
Rudofsky B, 1969 *Streets for People* (Garden City, N Y: Doubleday)
Ruskin J, n.d. *The Seven Lamps of Architecture* (New York: E R Dumont)
Sandford J, Law R, 1967 *Synthetic Fun* (Harmondsworth: Penguin Books)
St Exupery A de, 1940 *Wind, Sand and Stars* (New York: Harcourt, Brace and World)
St Exupery A de, 1943 *The Little Prince* (New York: Harcourt, Brace and World)
St Lawrence Parks Commission, n.d. Upper Canada Village (tourist brochure)
Sartre J-P, 1948 *L'Etre et le Néant* (Paris: Gallimard)
Sauer C, 1963 "The morphology of landscape" in *Land and Life: A Selection from
    the Writings of Carl Ortwin Sauer* Ed J Leighly (Berkeley: University of California
    Press)
Schütz A, 1962 *Collected Papers* Volumes I and II (The Hague: Martinus Nijhoff)
Schütz A, 1967 "Phenomenology and the social sciences" in *Phenomenology: The
    Philosophy of Edmund Husserl* Ed J J Kockelmans (Garden City, N Y: Doubleday)
Scott G, 1961 *The Architecture of Humanism* (London: Methuen)
Scully V, 1962 *The Earth, The Temple and The Gods: Greek Sacred Architecture*
    (New Haven: Yale University Press)
Seeley J R, Sim R A, Loosley E W, 1956 *Crestwood Heights* (Toronto: University of
    Toronto Press)
Shepard P, 1967 *Man in the Landscape* (New York: Ballantine Books)
Sissman L E, 1971 "The bus-line in the sky and other expensive indignities" *Atlantic
    Monthly* September pp 34-35
Snow J T, 1967 "The New Road in the United States" *Landscape* 17 13-16
Spiegelberg H, 1965 "The essentials of the phenomenological method" off print of
    Chapter XIV *The Phenomenological Movement* (The Hague: Martinus Nijhoff)
Spivak M, 1973 "Archetypal place" in *Environmental Design Research* Ed F E Preiser
    Proceedings of 4th EDRA Conference (Stroudsberg, Pa: Dowden, Hutchinson
    and Ross)
Stegner W, 1962 *Wolf-Willow* (New York: The Viking Press)

Steinbeck J, 1969 *The Grapes of Wrath* (New York: Bantam)
Strabo, 1917-1932 *The Geography of Strabo* translated by R L Jones (London: Heinemann)
Strasser S, 1967 "Phenomenology and the human sciences" in *Phenomenology: The Philosophy of Edmund Husserl* Ed J J Kockelmans (Garden City, N Y: Doubleday)
Swinburne R, 1968 *Space and Time* (London: Macmillan)
Taylor N, 1973 *The Village in the City* (London: Temple Smith)
Tillich P, 1958 in *Four Existentialist Theologians* Ed W Herberg (Garden City, N Y: Doubleday)
Tocqueville A de, 1945 *Democracy in America* Volume II (New York: Vintage Books)
Toffer A, 1970 *Future Shock* (New York: Bantam)
Trilling L, 1971 *Sincerity and Authenticity* (Cambridge, Mass: Harvard University Press)
Tuan Yi-fu, 1961 "Topophilia—or sudden encounter with landscape" *Landscape* 11 29-32
Tuan Yi-fu, 1969 *China* (Chicago: Aldine)
Tuan Yi-fu, 1971 "Geography, phenomenology and the study of human nature" *Canadian Geographer* 25 181-192
Tuan Yi-fu, 1974 *Topophilia* (Englewood Cliffs, N J: Prentice-Hall)
Tuan Yi-fu, 1975 "Space and place: Humanistic perspective" in *Progress in Geography* Volume 6 (London: Edward Arnold)
Turnbull C M, 1965 *Wayward Servants* (Garden City, N Y: Natural History Press)
Tymieniecka A-T, 1962 *Phenomenology and Science in Contemporary European Thought* (no place of publication given: Noonday Press)
Venturi R, 1966 *Complexity and Contradiction in Architecture* Museum of Modern Art Papers on Architecture 1 (New York: Museum of Modern Art)
Venturi R, Brown D S, 1972 *Learning from Las Vegas* (Cambridge, Mass: MIT Press)
Vidal de la Blache P, 1913 "Des caractères distinctifs de la géographie" *Annales de Géographie* 22 289-299
Vycinas V, 1961 *Earth and Gods* (The Hague: Martinus Nijhoff)
Wagner P L, 1972 *Environments and Peoples* (Englewood Cliffs N J: Prentice-Hall)
Webber M M, 1964 "The urban place and the nonplace urban realm" in *Explorations into Urban Structure* Ed M M Webber (Philadelphia: University of Pennsylvania Press)
Weil S, 1955 *The Need for Roots* (Boston: Beacon Press)
Whitman W, 1959 "Years of the Modern" in *Complete Poetry and Selected Prose* Ed J E Miller (Cambridge, Mass: The Riverside Press)
Whittlesey D, 1935 "The impress of effective central authority upon the landscape" *Annals* (Association of American Geographers) 25 (2) 85-97
Wild J, 1955 *The Challenge of Existentialism* (Bloomington: Indiana University Press)
Wild J, 1959 "Man and his lived-world" in *For Roman Ingarden* (The Hague: Martinus Nijhoff)
Wingo L, (Ed), 1963 *Cities and Space* (Baltimore: Johns Hopkins University Press)
Wright A T, 1942 *Islandia* (New York: Signet Books)
Wright J K, 1947 "Terrae Incognitae: The place of imagination in geography" *Annals* (Association of American Geographers) 37 1-15
Young I, 1969 "Cold comfort" in *Notes from a Native Land* Ed A Wainwright (Ottawa: Oberon Press)
Zelinsky W, 1973 *The Cultural Geography of the United States* (Englewood Cliffs, NJ: Prentice Hall)

Index

Abbau 114
Absurdity 127
Architecture 24, 35, 73, 77-78, 92-93, 126, 134
Aristotle 24
Assimilation/accommodation 59-60
Australian Aborigines 14-15, 65
Authenticity 64, 67, 71, 80, 117, 145-146

Bachelard G 11, 20, 49
Barthes R 85, 129-130, 137-139

Camus A 11, 37, 46-47, 114, 127
Care 18, 37-39, 142
Central authority 114-115, 144
Centres (of existence) 11, 15-16, 18, 21-22, 39, 42-43, 49-50, 142
Chartres 73
Community 33-36, 57-58
Consciousness (see also experience) 6, 34, 42-43, 124
Corporations 35, 109-114, 134
Cox H 40, 63, 65, 68, 143, 144-145
Cullen G 18, 35, 50, 52, 53-54, 79, 146

Dardel E 5, 10-11, 16, 41, 48, 128
Dasein 64
Design process 67-68, 145-146
Disneyfication 95-101, 128
Distinctiveness i, 31, 44-45, 48, 68, 134, 139
Diversity i, 46, 117, 145-146
Dubos R 30-31, 37, 48
Dwelling 17-18, 28, 39, 146

Economic system 115-117
Eliade M 15-16, 18, 49
Ellul J 81, 115-116
Everyday life 6, 29, 39, 41, 131-132
Existence 5, 17-18, 39-41, 43
Experience ii, 4-7, 10-11, 15-16, 36, 47, 50, 64, 66, 136, 140-141

Fixes 122
Flatscape 79, 117
Functional circle 8, 48
Futurisation 103-105

Gauldie S 1, 22, 23, 60, 65-66, 77-78, 83, 147
Genius Loci 48, 66

Geography 1-6, 11, 20, 34, 51, 58, 89, 131, 140, 141, 147
  phenomenological basis of 4-7, 10-11
  placeless 90, 117-121, 141

Heidegger M 1, 5, 17-18, 28, 31, 38-39, 40, 45, 64, 78, 143, 146
Home 9, 20, 31, 33, 39-40, 55, 77, 82-83, 143
Howard Johnson's 112, 114, 143

Identity (of places and landscapes) 24, 28, 31, 33, 41, 44-62, 65-66, 133, 134
Images 18-20, 56
  consensus 58-59
  group or community 57-58
  individual 56-57
  mass 57
  public 58
Inauthenticity 78-82, 133
Insideness 35, 49, 65, 142
  behavioural 53-54
  empathetic 54-55, 60
  existential 55-56, 60, 62
  incidental 51
  vicarious 52-53
Intentionality 10, 12, 16, 28, 31, 42-43, 47, 50, 66, 123
Intersubjectivity 9, 12, 21, 44, 45, 57
I-Thou, I-You 65-66, 73, 78

Jackson J B 93, 126, 131

Kierkegaard S 125-126
Kitsch 82, 90, 95

Landscape 5, 11, 15, 17, 20, 30-31, 33-34, 36, 42, 48, 79, 90, 105, 122
  absurd 127-128
  everyday 131-133
  present-day 122-125
  protean 133-135
  rational 125-127, 133
  simple 135-137
  theoretical 116
Lefebvre H 41-42, 126, 129, 131
Lifton R J 40, 109, 127, 131, 133
Lived-world i, 6, 12, 43
Location 3-5, 24, 29-30, 37, 46, 51
Lynch K 18, 35, 45, 71

Marcel G 43, 49
Mass culture 57, 68, 80-81, 92, 114
Mass media 58, 60, 90-92, 134, 143
Meaning (see significance)
Mobility 29-30, 83, 135
Museumisation 101-103, 145
Myths 137-139

New towns 126
Non-place urban realm 52, 120
Norberg-Schulz C 1, 20, 22, 25-26, 42,
    49, 67, 79, 124

Ontario Place 104, 105, 136-137
Other-directedness 93, 109
Outsideness 31, 49
    existential 51, 60, 62
    incidental 52
    objective 51-52

Paths 10, 20-21
Phenomenology ii, 4-7
Place i, 1-6, 9, 11-12, 20-30, 42, 53, 78,
    141-143
    and community 33-36
    and landscape 30-31
    and location 29-30
    and time 31-33
    drudgery of 41
    essence of 42-43
    private 36-37
    public 34-38
Placelessness ii, 6, 30, 63, 71, 79, 90, 122,
    139, 143
Place-making 67-78, 142-147
Place names 16-17
Placeness 35
Planning i, 22-23, 52, 81, 87-89, 109,
    126, 136
Pornscape 95
Primitive cultures 9, 12, 60, 65, 68, 83
Proteanism 133-134
Pseudo-places 58, 93

Rationalism 125-126
Renaissance 22-23, 35, 73-75
Rootedness (roots) 18, 37-39, 41, 76,
    146

Schütz A 6, 10, 12, 20
Seeing 54
Selective vision 123-124

Selfconsciousness 9-10, 18, 24, 51, 64, 67,
    71, 82, 145-146
Sense of place 2, 31, 48-49, 52-53, 63-78,
    82, 103, 117, 145
Significance 10, 17, 18, 20, 42, 137-139,
    140
Sincerity 63-64
SLOIP 23, 108
Space 3, 5, 8-28, 81, 87
    abstract 25-26
    architectural 22-24, 30
    cognitive 24-25
    Euclidean 24-25
    existential or lived 12-22
    geographical 16-22, 120
    mental 49-50
    perceptual 9-12
    planning 22-24
    pragmatic 8-9
    primitive 8-9
    profane 12-13
    sacred 12-13, 15-16, 65
    structure of 9-10, 18-22, 50
Sparing 18, 38-39, 146
Spirit of place (see also sense of place) 31,
    48-49
Standardisation (see uniformity)
Subtopia 105-106
Suburbia 18, 71, 92, 105, 123, 126, 132,
    134, 136
Symbols 137

Taliesin West 77-78
Technique 81, 87-89, 115, 117, 143-144
Time 31-33
Topophilia 37-123
Toronto 108, 113, 119, 128, 134, 136-137
Tourism 59, 83-87, 92, 93
Townscape 17, 53
Tradition 32-33
Trobriand Islands 12-14
Tuan Y-F 2, 3, 5, 9, 11, 37, 54, 137

Uniformity 15, 18, 79, 92, 109, 114-116,
    132, 134-135, 143
Uniqueness 3, 44, 48-49, 54, 56, 61
Unselfconsciousness 6, 8-9, 12, 18, 60,
    64-65, 68, 82

Venturi R 131-133, 136

Wagner P 34, 44, 92